D1714662

YOUNG TRAVELERS TO JERUSALEM

AN ANNOTATED SURVEY OF
AMERICAN AND ENGLISH JUVENILE LITERATURE
ON THE HOLY LAND
1785–1940

"'IT IS BETTER TO RIDE TO BETHLEHEM DONKEY BACK'"

Wade, *Twin Travelers in the Holy Land* (1919)

JOSEPH SHADUR

YOUNG TRAVELERS TO JERUSALEM

AN ANNOTATED SURVEY OF
AMERICAN AND ENGLISH JUVENILE LITERATURE
ON THE HOLY LAND
1785–1940

THE INGEBORG RENNERT CENTER FOR JERUSALEM STUDIES
BAR ILAN UNIVERSITY
RAMAT GAN
1999

Published by
Joseph Shadur
P.O. Box 4704, 91046 Jerusalem
under the auspices of
The Ingeborg Rennert Center for Jerusalem Studies,
Bar Ilan University, 52900 Ramat Gan, Israel

U.S. Distribution: Schoen Books,
Old Firehouse, So. Deerfield, MA 01373

ISBN: 965-222-919-9

Cover design adapted by Yehudit Shadur from *Ned Harwood's Travels* (1888)

Printed in Israel
Typesetting, printing, and binding: Keterpress Enterprises, Jerusalem

In memory of Rafi

The Ingeborg Rennert Center for Jerusalem Studies at Bar Ilan University is an interdisciplinary institute devoted to all aspects of Jerusalem's history, culture, and religion—past and present. The Rennert Center undertakes an extensive range of studies and research projects. Alongside its academic objectives, a popular outreach program of lectures, symposia, colloquia, and conferences brings the message of Jerusalem to the public at large, both in Israel and the Diaspora.

The Ingeborg Rennert Center for Jerusalem Studies welcomes the opportunity of extending academic sponsorship to Joseph Shadur's study of American and English juvenile books on the Holy Land, 1785–1940. Whereas Hebrew juvenile literature is a subject of scholarly scrutiny in Israel, assessment of writing for children and youngsters in other languages, as a contribution to the religious, social, and political history of the Land of Israel and Jerusalem, has not been noted in relevant scholarship until now. Joseph Shadur's groundbreaking research presents a wealth of significant information, and provides a sound basis for further academic studies in this field.

Prof. Joshua Schwartz

Director
The Ingeborg Rennert Center
for Jerusalem Studies

CONTENTS

ILLUSTRATIONS

MAPS

FOREWORD

THE STUDY before us dealing with American and English books for children and youngsters set in the Holy Land throws light on cultural and social factors that transcend the definition of "juvenile literature." In these pages, the close look at the books on this subject that appeared in Britain and the United States between 1785 and 1940 reveals fascinating interconnections of literature, theology, history, education for values, and even politics, in the periods during which these works were written.

Palestine—the Land of Israel, the Holy Land—was always far more than just another geographic and national concept. Throughout its very long human history, because of its particular geopolitical attributes, this small, semi-arid strip of land was frequently at the core of power struggles and wars for its possession. The cradle of Judaism and Christianity was endowed with added significance by the third monotheistic creed when the region was conquered by Arab Muslim forces and integrated in the Islamic world in the 7th century—albeit with relatively short-lived interludes of limited Christian control during the Middle Ages. The First World War was followed by another, brief, interlude of Christian rule: the British Mandate over Palestine.

Permeating the majority of the books surveyed here is the Christian conception that Palestine is primarily the land of Jesus that was usurped by Muslim Saracens and Turks. To the extent that Jews are mentioned (the land of the Bible was after all their country during First and Second Temple times) they generally appear as individuals, pitiful and barely tolerated, in disadvataged positions compared to the dominant Muslims, and to Christians who basked in the prominence of the European powers. Christian theological tradition regarded the dispersed and long-suffering Jews as living testimony to divine retribution for their rejection of Jesus as the Messiah. Their inferior state underlined the victory of Christianity. The redemption of the Jews would only come about with their recognition of the Christian Messiah.

While several of the children's books surveyed here also describe the Arab inhabitants of the Holy Land, the religion of Islam has virtually no place in this literature, most of which aimed—explicitly or implicitly—at making its young readers better Christians by identifying with the heroes of the narratives in their peregrinations, adventures, and other activities in Bible lands. The main guide-book that accompanied both adults and children in most of these works was the Bible—the New as well as the Old Testament.

Although through the years, under the influence of the changes in social structures and education, these books also underwent a certain measure of secularization most of them continued to reflect Christian theological outlooks, as is clearly brought out in the many passages quoted by the author. Unlike in books on other parts of the globe, most of the travelers and tourists moving through the Bible lands in these pages showed no great interest in the country's inhabitants and the conditions of their life—except as illustrative of Biblical scenes: The people of Palestine were secondary to the places sanctified by Biblical associations. Palestine was perceived as a sort of heavenly holy land, linked only incidentally to the down-to-earth country through which the Western visitors wound their way.

The study raises an important point touching on the definition of juvenile literature. Many of the writers introduce material culled from travel books written for adults on these regions. Thus, also in keeping with the educational aims and values in the English-speaking world during most of the period under review, there is not always a clear delimitation between works for children and those written for adults on this subject. The intense desire to bestow prevailing social and religious values on the younger generation caused many of these books to be loaded-down with details and subject matter that today would have been avoided in consideration of the developmental levels and absorptive capacity of young readers. Throughout much of the period under review children were regarded as miniature adults who had to be conditioned for life as good citizens, and particularly as good Protestant Christians.

The survey begins with an introductory chapter giving concise cultural, religious, and historical background overviews for the century-and-a-half under discussion, and relates to the imagined and more realistic conceptions of the Holy Land as seen through Western eyes by contemporaries. The main section of the book analyzes the different approaches of authors in presenting these conceptions (more often, preconceptions) to their young readers. This part is essentially chronological, reflecting the changing cultural conventions and stylistic fashions of the times against the background of relevant historical developments. Another chapter deals with the impressions of authors who personally lived in the Holy Land as children, and with observations by some of the writers of contemporary children native to "Bible lands." The concluding chapters draw generalized conclusions of the factors common to all of this writing, and probe the ideological conceptualizations and social conventions behind it. The numerous illustrations and quoted passages place this literature nicely into its period settings.

The extensive bibliographical sections at the end of the book reveal the scope of such writing and the relative popularity of English-language children's books set in the Holy Land. This meticulously gathered and collated information—as indeed the very presentation of the entire subject—is of considerable value as a foundation for further studies in different directions and of related topics: comparisons with Arabic and Hebrew (and perhaps Yiddish?) juvenile works dealing with the same geographical regions and countries; studies of similar literature in the periods subsequent to the 1930s and how it reflects the developing Jewish-Arab conflict and Western cultural influences; stylistic developments in the language of dialogues and descriptions of these countries' realities; how Bible lands are presented to youngsters in English-speaking countries—and elsewhere—today; the extent to which contemporary juvenile literature sheds light on the struggle between Palestinians and Israelis and its relevance to present realities; etc. For in our day still, despite all the momentous historic changes and modern developments in the Middle East, the children's literature of the region reflects religious/theological and national ideologies—be they Zionist/Socialist-motivated, ultra-Orthodox Jewish, latter-day Zionist, or more-or-less religiously-inspired Palestinian Muslim and Christian reading for children. A study of these "educational" children's books is also interesting from the point of view of adults reading books not written for them.

I do not know to what extent the books we read as children affect and condition our adult lives. I doubt that there is much direct evidence for this, or that such things are measurable. But as the author concludes, some significant effects are certainly conceivable—and probably more so in the pre-multimedia times examined here.

Menahem Regev
Jerusalem

PREFACE

During a prolonged stay in New England some years ago, I happened to come across a number of old books on the Holy Land written for children. Although I had occasionally found such books in Britain and elsewhere, I had never seen so many in so concentrated a time and area. My surprise was unwarranted: Many of the authors were from Massachusetts, and Boston publishers are amply represented on the title pages. Nor was the subject foreign to New England's Bible-steeped culture. At first, I was amused by the romantic and fanciful ways in which the landscapes, the people, and the local color of Palestine are presented in these works. But then, reading this material in the light of the modern history and realities of the Middle East elicited both smiles and gasps of disbelief, for these self-proclaimed educational books blithely flaunt stereotypes and prejudices—social, racial, ethnic, religious, and environmental—that are appalling by today's standards.

Indeed, such conventions also characterized much contemporaneous writing for young people on other topics, and particularly books of travel and encounters with far-away peoples. However, the particular works surveyed here, covering roughly a century-and-a-half from 1785 to 1940, accompanied the entry of the "Scripture Lands" into modern times. They present a revealing angle of

European and American vision on Muslim and Christian Arabs, Turks, Eastern and Western Christians, and Jews in the Holy Land and the adjacent countries during a period when the seeds of the present conflicts were being sown.

Although there are also a few earlier juvenile publications touching on the Holy Land, such children's books began to appear at a time when the memories of Napoleon Bonaparte's occupation of Egypt and his campaign in Palestine in the last years of the 18th century were still very much alive. From the 1820s on, they were produced in increasing numbers. This literature reflects the growing involvement of the European powers and America in the Middle East during the 19th century—through the First World War, and into the British Mandate over Palestine—and here and there echoes the beginnings of Arab nationalism and the inception of the Zionist movement. These were not isolated works, but a steady stream of books that deserve recognition as a distinct category in the vast corpus of "Palestiniana" literature. The appended bibliography lists about 160 titles, not counting various editions of the same works or books in languages other than English.

In portraying, describing, and attempting to categorize such children's books I have tried to share the blend of interest and distaste that these quaint works aroused in me, and venture generalizations as to their broader social implications. After making due allowance for the more fatuous aspects of current popular literary fashions, this literature can be rather charming and sometimes unintentionally very funny. If I quote from the original texts at some length, it is to convey their special flavor. This material adds specialized insights to the study of juvenile literature, and to library science and bibliographical listings, generally. But it will undoubtedly speak more meaningfully to those whose interests extend to the lands of the Middle East and their modern history, and more particularly to those with some acquaintance of Palestine travel literature. I might add that my presentation is avowedly one-sided. In pointing up common Western prejudices and attitudes, I do not suggest that—to the extent it exists—educational and didactic writing by Muslims, Jews, or Eastern Christians aspires to any greater objectivity regarding the European powers and their populations. A comparison would be illuminating.

The appended list of the works consulted and of items I was not actually able to see constitutes, to my knowledge, a first tentative bibliography of Christian juvenile books on the Holy Land (stopping short of illustrated Bible stories and religious textbooks for children, which are legion). Information on additional publications, especially in other languages, will contribute to a more definitive listing and may conceivably modify some of the overall impressions and conclusions.

I am grateful to Joseph Glass, Jeff Halper, Ruth Kark, Alan Paris, Ruth Roded, and Michael Swirsky for their apt comments and suggestions. I owe a special debt of gratitude to Menahem Regev who unstintingly shared with me his wide-ranging acquaintance of childrens' books and his extensive library, and helped crystallize my interpretations. My wife, Yehudit, was there at all stages with perceptions, advice, research, and infinite patience. I thank Gideon Hermel, Eliahu Hacohen, and Nathan Schur for some of the titles; Jean Carter for allowing me to reproduce parts of the McKenzie diary; and the library staff members of Amherst College and the University of Massachusetts at Amherst, Smith College and the Forbes Library at Northampton, the Boston Public Library, the New York Public Library Rare Book Department, the Library of Congress, and the British Library for their assistance in locating some of the less accessible material.

Jerusalem,
October 1998

INTRODUCTION

AMONG the innumerable works of travel, exploration, religion, and fiction dealing with the Holy Land that appeared throughout the 19th century and in the first decades of the 20th century are also books written for children and youngsters.[1] The great American-Jewish bibliographer, Abraham S.W. Rosenbach (1876–1952), who was an avid collector of juvenile literature, firmly believed that children's books had "…as much scholarly and bibliographical interest as books in other fields," and that "more than any class of literature they reflect the minds of the generation that produced them. Hence no better guide to the history and development of any country can be found.…" And he quotes William Godwin, the early 19th-century English publisher and writer of children's books: "It is children that read children's books, when they read, but it is parents who choose them."[2]

English books written specially for children first appeared in the mid-17th century and were exclusively religious: Even the most innocuous elements of fantasy and imagination were considered frivolous and unsuitable for young minds. With the great majority of children's books produced for profit, publishers and authors endeavored to satisfy a public that was long perceived as predicating puritan moral and religious attitudes.[3] It took a hundred years for the generally dour devotional motifs to be mitigated by more secular and recreational themes. But most books avowedly aiming to entertain as well as to instruct young readers only date from the early 19th century.[4] At least in the earlier part of the century but also later, as a reaction to new writing for children in a lighter vein in England, American influence tended to reinforce a more conservative approach in Britain—characterized by one authority as "a creeping paralysis of seriousness, which set in long before Victoria came to the throne."[5] On the whole, however, during the protracted period under review (1785–1940), the juvenile literature of the English-speaking countries underwent a gradual transformation. It can be traced from overwhelmingly didactic, religious, and moral writing with strong puritan and evangelical overtones, through books whose chief objective was to provide enjoyment while stimulating interest, study, and character development, to books written purely for children's amusement.

With fundamentalist evangelicalism, including also millenarian and messianic manifestations, thriving in 19th-century America and Britain, it should not be surprising that a religious-moralizing approach be particularly in evidence in children's books dealing with the Holy Land—the scene of the Second Coming. It was the publication of exciting new discoveries in "Scripture Lands" early in the 19th century, which were seen also as advancing Christian messianic aspirations, that inspired the introduction of adventure motifs into this literature. Only toward the end of the century did secular adventure and travel writing prevail in children's books set in the Middle East, with religious themes receiving at best perfunctory treatment. Nevertheless, evangelically-inspired stories of this kind persisted well into the 20th century.

Among the authors of the works surveyed here were some well-known literary figures writing for the young, but also a considerable proportion of men and women about whom no information seems to be readily available today. Quite a few were clergymen of various Protestant denominations and many women from a background in teaching and education, most of them of a decided evangelizing bent—including several missionaries. Some of them had no personal experience of the Bible lands they tell about; most had at least a fleeting acquaintance as tourists; a small minority actually lived in Palestine for extended periods. On the whole, these were solid, God-fearing people. Skepticism and religion do not go hand-in-hand, and so, even those books emphasizing adventure and heroic deeds in Bible lands never cross the line of acceptable religious and moral propriety, and none of these works are in the least polemical or go against the mainstream Protestant consensus.

It is axiomatic that at all times most private publishers are primarily concerned with profits, with the potential market for their products ever in their considerations. As the demand for exclusively religious and didactic writing waned toward the mid-19th century, the buying public's preferences may be gauged ultimately by the fact that those books which had a relatively greater entertainment coefficient were generally the ones that proved profitable enough to warrant further editions.[6]

The religious and cultural setting

Before entering into detailed, largely anecdotal descriptions of such children's books produced in the course of a century-and-a-half of religious, social, and political evolution, it is well to place this literature in its relevant historical and theological perspective and so provide terms of reference for assessing it as a social and cultural symptom.[7] Since by virtue of their subject matter—the "Scripture lands"—most of these little works were directly or indirectly inspired by religious concerns, they reflect theological trends current in America and England throughout this long period.

Protestant teaching, in general, emphasized salvation by faith in the atonement of Jesus, and by preaching and good works, rather than by the efficacy of the sacraments. In the latter part of the 18th and in the early 19th century, puritan evangelicalism, while obviously more dominant in New England, crucially affected religious developments in Britain—in the established Anglican as well as the Nonconformist churches. By the beginning of the Victorian

3

era evangelicalism transcended all sectarian denominations. In practice, if not formally, it was the religion of the court and pervaded all of British society down to the working classes. It widely implanted cultural constraints such as Sabbath (Sunday) observance, family prayers, and censorship. In America, in addition to influential Congregationalist, Presbyterian, Episcopalian, Methodist, Baptist, and Unitarian church organizations, the 1830s and 1840s saw the appearance of fundamentalist sects such as the Church of Latter Day Saints (Mormons) and the Millerites. As described through the eyes of some of their younger members in the following pages (under "American youngsters in Jaffa"), a few of these messianic Christians even attempted to settle in the Holy Land as an extreme manifestation of their beliefs.

The first American missionary, Jonas King, was followed by Pliny Fisk and Levi Parsons who were sent to Palestine and Syria in the early 1820s by the American Board of Commissioners for Foreign Missions founded at the Andover Theological Seminary in 1810. They were succeeded throughout the 19th century by a constantly swelling stream of such men and women, many of them looked after by American consular representatives and the State Department. English and Scottish medical and educational missions in intimate contact with the British Foreign Office paralleled these efforts. In 1841 the Church of England established a Protestant Bishopric of Jerusalem, initially as a joint venture of the British and Prussian governments. These activities were predicated on the basic Christian belief that the destruction of the Jewish commonwealth, the dispersion of the Jews among the nations of the world, and their sufferings, represented divine retribution for their rejection of the true Messiah. The restoration of the Jews to their ancient homeland in Palestine, and their conversion, would herald the Millennium—the Second Coming of Jesus.

The evangelicalist belief that life on earth was only important as preparation for eternity induced highly sophisticated people to put pleasure in the background and elevate duty and purpose as the guiding principles of life. In the constant quest for self-improvement "useful knowledge" was equated with "Christian knowledge." The Society for the Promotion of Christian Knowledge (S.P.C.K.) was founded in the late 18th century; the British and the Scottish Church Missionary Societies (C.M.S.) celebrated their 50–year jubilee in 1848; the Christian Tract Society and the London Society for Promoting Christianity Amongst the Jews (L.J.S.) were both established in 1809; the American Sunday School Union (A.S.S.U.) in the 1820s. Self-imposed sense of mission engendered superiority—a deep-felt conviction that the "English-speaking people…" bore great responsibility "…in deciding the destinies of mankind."[8] Increasingly fashionable travel in parts of Asia and Africa by the upper classes and industrial and commercial *nouveaux riches* reinforced (disdainful) concern for "lesser breeds" and "benighted" peoples who ought to be enlightened and morally prepared by missionaries for receiving the benefits of Western civilization.

The post-Civil War decades saw a tremendous growth of American missionary activity abroad. In the 1890s the Congregationalists alone had over a hundred missionaries in the Ottoman empire with over 70,000 proselytes—mostly from among the local Eastern Christian populations.[9] Sermons and religious periodicals frequently expressed ideas of racial superiority and portrayed the nation's expansion as the ordained will of the Almighty. From the 1870s on—under the impact of the growing emphasis on their overseas empires by England, and later the United States—puritan religious fervor became gradually transmuted into the humanitarian concerns of evangelicalist Christianity. But having bred the anti-slavery (abolitionist), child-labor reform, and temperance movements, in time it also took on imperialist and nationalistic attributes. At the high tide of British imperialism and *fin-de-siècle* hedonism, the interest in religious literature waned, and this too left its mark on the character of the children's books and periodicals of the two decades preceding the First World War and thereafter.

Although each of the two Anglo-Saxon "cousin" nations was subject to its own dynamics—and these were certainly not identical—there had always been close and constant communication and

5

interchange between them, even throughout the periods of Anglo-American tension following the American Revolution, and during the War of 1812 and the American Civil War. Editions of the same books were published (and copyrights often unabashedly pirated) on both sides of the Atlantic, and their periodicals read by each other. Among the joint societies formed in the 19th century was the Anglo-American Committee and the outspokenly anti-Catholic Evangelical Alliance. In the cultural sphere "Anglo-Saxon" affinities drew on common evangelicalist roots in dealing with moral issues—spreading the puritan world-view in its various interpretations by missionaries at home and abroad, and addressing the problem of slavery; the restoration of Jews to their ancient land as an essential precondition for the Second Advent; current issues such as the Armenian Question; and generally inculcating the Protestant work ethic.

This community of interests intensified toward the end of the 19th century as America asserted its place among the leading imperialist powers. Throughout the 19th century, the religious connotations of the Holy Land were increasingly compounded by foreign policy considerations (the Eastern Question; commercial and strategic objectives; etc.) and by what was perceived as the national interest. Public pronouncements proclaimed the "Anglo-Saxon Race," with its "instinct or genius for colonizing" to be commissioned by divine providence to be "his brother's keeper."[10] And in terms of the power politics in the Middle East, the British Colonial Secretary, Joseph Chamberlain, summed up a speech in 1898 with: "Who would provoke a combination of the two Anglo-Saxon nations…bring[ing] irresistible force to bear in defense of the weak and oppressed? The mere fact of their alliance would…bring the Sultan to his knees."[11]

In these childrens' books on the Holy Land one looks in vain for some echo of the liberal and anti-imperialist opinion that existed as a vocal political and intellectual undercurrent, especially in the years around the turn of the 20th century. In Great Britain its influential protagonists included men like William E. and Herbert Gladstone, Richard Cobden, Wilfrid Scaven Blunt, John Morley,

George Bernard Shaw, and J.A. Hobson; in the United States, leading public and literary figures such as William Jennings Bryan, Carl Schurz, E.L. Godkin of the *Nation*, William James, Mark Twain, and many others held parallel opinions. That such sentiments are absent in "educational" writing on the Holy Land and Bible-related subjects for children is, however, not really surprising: At the time, most religious establishments—Catholic as well as Protestant—vociferously championed their respective (White) nations' "God-imposed responsibilities as civilizing agents." America and England were the instruments for the advancement of Christian civilization.

Such attitudes devolved from the top echelons of society, the universities, churches, theological colleges, and the plethora of Sunday schools. They were spread widely by the growth of religious and secular journalism. The children's books we leaf through here reflect the outlooks of their authors, and the concepts generally held by the parents, relatives, family friends, and educators who bought them. Because of the conscious persistence of puritan Christian values in educational literature, even when England and America were moving toward greater "scientific" secularism, we must not look for absolute consistency with the culture at large in these works. And indeed, as is borne out by the dozens of anecdotal examples adduced below, the commonly-held social attitudes and prejudices come through clearly enough.

The historical context

The involvement of the Western powers in the Middle East in the 19th and the early 20th century was primarily a British historical phenomenon, less so French, and later also German. It began with Napoleon Bonaparte's endeavors at cutting England's routes to India by occupying Egypt in 1798, and after the destruction of the French fleet in Aboukir Bay by Nelson, attempting to conquer Syria and the Ottoman empire. On the way, the French took El Arish and Jaffa, but their siege of Acre in 1799 was foiled by the energetic defense of the garrison under Ahmed "al-Djezzar" Pasha, reinforced by Ottoman contingents and Royal Navy units commanded by Sir Sidney Smith. The retreat of the French from Palestine marked the turning point in their Egyptian venture. However, the work of the French scholars and scientists who accompanied the army to Egypt and Palestine aroused immediate interest in the antiquities of the region. It was one of the main factors in prompting the scholarly and scientific exploration and "rediscovery" of the Bible lands by the West, from the early 1800s on.

In 1831, Muhammad-Ali, the modernizing, semi-autonomous viceroy of Ottoman Egypt invaded Palestine, Lebanon, and Syria and defeated the sultan's forces in eastern Anatolia. Great Britain, France, and several of the European powers who saw it in their interest to help the Turkish sultan maintain Ottoman hegemony, forced Muhammad-Ali to evacuate Syria and Palestine in 1840–41. But the near-decade of Egyptian rule opened the conservative Muslim administration of the country to Western influences, including safer movement of travelers, pilgrims, and tourists, and a rapidly growing, permanent foreign presence. In the Crimean War of 1853–56 Britain and other European powers fought on the Turkish side against Russia and were profoundly concerned in the intensification of internal reforms which had been started by the Porte in the 1820s, and in the economic penetration of the Ottoman domain. A direct consequence of continuous Western influence and involvement in the Ottoman empire was a rapidly growing increase in the physical presence of West Europeans and Americans (and also Russians) in Palestine and Syria—missionaries, consular and church representatives, settlers, businessmen, commercial agents, professional persons, pilgrims, and tourists. Partly as a reaction to this foreign influx and as a result of enhanced educational facilities, the nascent Arab nationalist movement was given further impetus by its reaction to overt imperialist intrusion into Egypt and subsequent Western domination of the country. The Suez Canal was completed in 1869. In 1875 Disraeli acquired the controlling shares in the Suez Canal Company for Great Britain, and in 1882 direct British military intervention in internal Egyptian politics crushed an Arab nationalist uprising led by Arabi Pasha and brought all of Egypt and northern Sinai under effective British control and administration. After initial failures in the mid-1880s, the Sudan was finally subdued by Kitchener in 1898. The British in Egypt gained full control over all of Sinai in 1906.

Unconnected with these developments, under the pressure of virulent anti-Jewish excesses in Russia, the year 1882 also marked the beginnings of Jewish proto-Zionist settlement in Palestine; the Zionist movement proper was founded in 1897. By now German ambitions in the Ottoman empire began to assume commercial, strategic, and even tactical importance, a much-publicized event being the ostentatious state visit of Kaiser Wilhelm II to Turkey, Syria, and Palestine in 1898. Arab nationalism reached new heights in the years preceding World War I in the wake of the Young Turks revolution and in opposition to the ensuing Turkification policies in the Ottoman empire. During World War I, two German and Turkish attacks on the Suez Canal across northern Sinai in 1915 and 1916 sparked a British counter-offensive from Egypt into Palestine and Syria under Murray's and later Allenby's command. Shortly before Jerusalem was conquered in December 1917 by Allenby's forces, Jewish aspirations to a national home in Palestine were given British governmental sanction in the Balfour Declaration. The Allied, mainly British, final drive to Damascus through northern Palestine in 1918 was accompanied to the east by the more-or-less sporadic actions of Bedouin Arab irregulars, romanticized by the T.E. Lawrence "legends." In 1920, after two years of military administration, Great Britain formally took over the government of Palestine and Transjordan under the League of Nations Mandate, and the force of Arab national feeling turned with increased vehemence against the Zionist advances—as well as against the British in Palestine and the French in Syria.

Holy Land perceptions and realities

Protestant Westerners whose education and cultural conditioning from early childhood was intensely Bible-oriented tended to form mental images of the Holy Land from widespread, commonplace

9

JERUSALEM.

Butterworth, *Zigzag Journeys in the Levant* (1886)

conceptions. Thus in their mind's eye the narrow, shallow Jordan was a mighty stream; barely trickling water sources—"fountains;" decaying towns—romantic, ivy-covered ruins out of classical Renaissance paintings; poor Arab fellahin scratching the soil with wooden plows—Biblical patriarchs. Even though many open-minded visitors portrayed the actual state of the country in innumerable books and articles, all too many descriptions, pictures, prints, and illustrations of the Holy Land tended to perpetuate idealized and sanitized visions of the country and its people.

In the latter centuries of Ottoman-Turkish rule, Palestine—Southern Syria—was hardly a "land flowing with milk and honey." Most of what we know today of its physical aspect and human geography in that pre-modern-development, pre-large-scale-irrigation age can be gleaned from the recorded impressions and observations of an ever-increasing stream of travelers, pilgrims, missionaries, explorers, and other foreigners who came to the region from the turn of the 19th century on. After rainy winters the largely rocky countryside and the plains looked green and fresh, with immense, if ephemeral, carpets of lovely wildflowers. But in drought years, and throughout the long, dry summer season most of the landscapes reverted to dull ochers, grays, and glaring whites that many transient visitors found depressing and forbidding. Even devout Christians whose preconceptions were conditioned by deep religious zeal—not to mention more cynically-inclined tourists—recoiled from what they saw.

Thus, for example, idealized visions of the Heavenly Jerusalem were quickly dispelled by the dismal neglect, poverty, and backwardness. Viewed from a distance (in 1820), the Holy City

> …presented a most inspiring aspect, but on entering all expectations of magnificence are shattered. Within the walls all is ruins, wretchedness, desolation, narrow streets, miserable bazaars, with a few relics of sculpture….and its inhabitants most filthy in dress and general appearance. Its six gates are regularly shut at the going down of the sun.[12]

A generation later, except for more openness to foreigners, things were not much better, and only from the mid-1850s and 1860s on— the final decades of Ottoman government—did modern improvements begin to appear. The population of Palestine increased steadily from about a quarter million at the turn of the 19th century to 800,000 on the eve of the First World War.

The multiplicity of rival Christian sects bedevilled the identification and access to holy places in Palestine. The main contenders were the Greek-Orthodox monks of the Brotherhood of the Holy Sepulcher who identified Christian holy sites according to their dogma, and the Roman Catholic ("Latin") Franciscan monks of the Custodia Terra Sancta who maintained the holy places sanctioned and recognized by the Vatican. Where they shared the same sites, as in the Church of the Holy Sepulcher and the Church of the Nativity in Bethlehem, Turkish soldiers were regularly posted at the entrance to check outbreaks of sectarian violence.

Standard travelers' routes are indicated by broken lines

Until proper tourist accommodations and hotels became available in the 1870s, Western Christian travelers resorted to monasteries and primitive pilgrims' hostels, or camped out in tents, rather than put up in local khans notorious for their vermin. Few attempted to travel on their own, and most tourists engaged the services of dragomans, or later of commercial travel agencies, to see to their needs along the way and to smooth passage through reputedly hostile regions and Bedouin tribal lands.

Tourists and pilgrims generally followed several standard itineraries, depending on the port where they disembarked. A popular, if costlier route covered Egypt from Alexandria to Cairo and up and down the Nile, and proceeded to Palestine either by boat to Jaffa, or sometimes by camel and mule caravan along the northern Sinai road to Gaza and Jaffa. In some cases, the Monastery of St. Catherine and Mount Sinai were visited as well. In Palestine, the common itinerary departed from Jaffa where ships had to anchor off-shore, and travelers with their baggage were rowed ashore through the surf by sturdy Arab boatmen to the small landing stage. Most rode on horseback and mules via Ramleh and Latrun into the Judean mountain country, past Abu Ghosh to Nabi Samwil, where a distant view of Jerusalem never failed to evoke tremors of religious excitement. Until the 1880s accommodations were almost exclusively within the Old City; later, also in the new western suburbs. Excursions from Jerusalem led past Rachel's Tomb to Bethlehem, occasionally to Solomon's Pools and back, and rarely even as far as Hebron. The other standard trip from the Holy City was to Jericho, the place of Baptism in the Jordan, and to the northern Dead Sea shore. From Jerusalem many travelers followed the road, or rather track, along the Samaria Mountains watershed line to Nablus, and proceeded from there by way of Jenin to Mount Tabor and Tiberias on the Sea of Galilee, or by way of Nazareth. From Galilee many continued to Lebanon and Damascus, and sailed from Beirut. Alternative routes began in Beirut and followed the same routes south to Jerusalem, and from there west to Jaffa. Only toward the end of the 19th century were the first proper roadways constructed and wheeled carriages introduced; from 1892 on, most travelers between Jaffa and Jerusalem went by train.

After the end of the Crimean War in 1856, under the capitulations system then in force giving certain foreign states extraterritorial rights in the Ottoman empire, communities of foreign Christian nationals and of Jews proliferated throughout Palestine, and most powers and lesser European states maintained consulates and consular agencies in Jerusalem and other towns. Many foreign religious, educational, charitable, and medical missionary establishments dotted the country, with the greatest concentration in and around Jerusalem. The main centers of Jewish life were the traditional holy cities of Tiberias, Safed, Jerusalem, and Hebron.

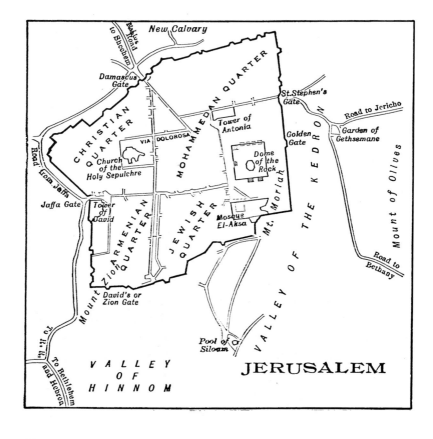

By the end of the 19th century increasing numbers of Jews lived also in Jaffa and Haifa; in Jerusalem they made up the majority of the population. New Jewish agricultural settlements ("colonies") began to appear in the country from the early 1880s on.

During the First World War Palestine was an active theater of hostilities and the population suffered greatly from hunger, disease, and deprivation. The conquest of Palestine and Syria by the Allies in 1917–18 ended Ottoman Turkish rule of the country. Temporary military administration brought relief, and after the establishment of the British Mandate over Palestine in 1920, well-ordered government and Zionist immigration led to a continuous population increase and relative prosperity accompanied, however, by successive outbreaks of Arab-Jewish violence. In 1936, the Arab population of Palestine rose in revolt against the British authorities, and sporadic internecine fighting continued until World War II.

Almost until the end of the period reviewed here, the native Muslim and Christian Arabs, Druze, and other traditional ethnic groupings of Palestine remained largely unaffected by the modernization and cosmopolitanization of the country. Impoverished, oppressed, illiterate villagers did not know what to make of rich Western tourists spending good money and going to considerable trouble for what seemed to them useless travel, just to look at old stones and gawk at the people. How was it that infidel Christian strangers were allowed to move about with impunity in a Muslim land? Why was it a punishable offence to attack them and take their property? All that was left to the locals was to try to earn a few coppers by serving the foreigners, and beg for baksheesh.

*

Very briefly, these are the key events, developments, and conditions that in various degrees are reflected and alluded to in the children's literature examined here. With the main focus of interest on the religious connotations of Bible lands, little, if any, regard in these works is directed at the contemporary history and circumstances of the peoples and countries dealt with, except as they affected Western visitors.

THE TOMB OF RACHEL.

Knox, *The Boy Travellers, Egypt and the Holy Land* (1882)

I

THE HOLY LAND FOR THE YOUNG:
WRITERS, SOURCES, PLOT CONSTRUCTIONS

JVENILE books touching on actual geographical and historical aspects of Scripture lands may be classified into several, often overlapping, categories: geographical texts usually compiled for Sunday schools; dramatizations for youngsters of historical or biblical events and personalities set in the Holy Land; fictitious adventure plots inspired by actual exploration and travels, and by military campaigns; travelogues taking imaginary, or sometimes real, young heroes along the usual tourist and pilgrim routes; and books based on actual, personal experiences of children in the Holy Land and in the adjacent countries. Of related interest are works and passages in books on Palestine and the Middle East that describe children and their activities. Each of these types of writing is examined below.

Although very many books for children on Old and New Testament Bible stories, Bible history, biblical personalities, and religious school texts were aimed at the same type of reading public, they are not directly relevant to the subject under discussion here and—except for a few examples emphasizing geography—are not included in this survey. Nor does the survey cover the numerous children's periodicals which occasionally contained articles on the Holy Land. A few of the titles give an indication of their import: *The Children's Magazine; Calculated for the Use of Families and Schools,* published for the General Protestant Episcopal Sunday School Union in Hartford, Connecticut from 1789 to at least 1874; *The Children's Friend* published in Pennsylvania and elsewhere; the *Juvenile Missionary Herald* of the London Baptist Missionary Society; the *Juvenile Missionary Magazine* of the United Presbyterian Missionary Board in Edinburgh and the Directors of the London Missionary Society; *The Youth's Companion; for All the Family*, which appeared in Boston for well over a century from 1827 on; the *St. Nicholas; A Magazine for Boys and Girls*, highly popular on both sides of the Atlantic and the English-speaking world generally from 1873 to 1939; etc. However, such literature certainly conformed to the social attitudes and outlooks discussed below.

The first half of the 19th century

Geographical compendiums and didactic plots

Books for "young persons" based on first-hand impressions of authors who had visited or lived in different countries began to appear in the late 18th century. At first these were mainly anthologies of chapters culled from the writings of various travelers, usually also including descriptions of the Middle Eastern lands. For example, *The Flowers of Modern Travels, etc.* first published in 1797 by the Reverend John Adams (1750?-1814) has excerpts from the writings of Mme. Savary, Baron de Tott, and Irwin on Egypt, and Lady Montagu on Turkey and Persia.[13] In the "Advertisement" to his two-volume compendium Adams declares that

> No books whatever are more instructive and entertaining than books of Travels. They are particularly well-adapted to young people. They satisfy that eager thirst for knowledge, which is found very strong in early life, and they interest the mind as much as a novel. They make it usefully inquisitive, and furnish it with matter for reflection.[14]

Mrs. Jamieson's *Popular Voyages and Travels, etc.* (1820) contains similar, more recent, material. Bringing first-hand observations of such writers into a more specifically religious setting "to occupy a place among those useful volumes which the young will be allured to read on the hallowed hours between the intervals of public worship on the Lord's Day...by the side of...Scripture Stories"[15] are books on the "Manners and Customs Peculiar to the East." The Quaker, Maria Hack (1777–1844) who wrote specifically for the young, at one point stated that "It may be doubted whether habituating children to seek amusement, almost exclusively, in fictitious narrative, has not a direct tendency to weaken the natural powers."[16] In her *Oriental Fragments* (1828) she quotes freely—in the verbose, florid manner of the period—from the accounts of "European travellers...esteemed for their general knowledge and accuracy of observation" like Pococke and Clarke[17] who traveled through Syria and Palestine. Hack's declared

> ...object was to instruct and amuse, by a faithful account of what [the travelers] deemed worthy of observation in the countries they describe so that for a great number of young persons...the study of the Scriptures will become more interesting, from opening a connexion between it and other branches of knowledge; and considering the inaptitude of many for receiving instruction of a character exclusively religious, it seems a duty to strengthen by every innocent means, associations which may lead to the happiest results.[18]

The Reverend Bourne Hall Draper's *Bible Illustrations* (1831, and several later English and American editions) convey the information in the form of loosely-constructed narrations by an adult relative or mentor to small children who ask the right leading questions ("Harry was a very sensible boy, and apt to ask questions about everything. His father encouraged him to do so....").[19]

A few works in this genre specifically describing the Holy Land are among the vast amount of material published by the American Sunday School Union (A.S.S.U.). This influential organization was founded in Philadelphia in 1824 by combining the resources of several Protestant denominations in order to establish a confederated system of religious education through oral instruction and publication of suitable reading material for school and home. Any enjoyment the youthful readers may have derived from these books must have been incidental to the propagandistic aims of this literature—on the principle that "religion is so far from being gloomy, that it renders its possessors cheerful in hours of great trial...."[20] These small-format booklets include *Selumiel, or, A Visit to Jerusalem* (1833) written in Andover by a young divinity student at the seminary, and *Uncle Austin and His Nephews*, published in 1838. Both are constructed as artificial, contrived plots built around tedious cathechistical question-and-answer dialogues on precepts of Christian moral conduct, the Bible, and biblical geography:

> *George Homer* [one of the boys in the class]. I should like to ask you, Mr. Anderson, whether the fountain of Siloam is still to be seen at Jerusalem.
> *Mr. Anderson* [the Sunday school teacher]. It is. Our American missionaries, Messrs. Fisk and King, visited Jerusalem in 1823, and have given a description of this fountain, which I will read to you....[21]

And:

> *Uncle*. Impress this point upon your mind, that *Sacred Geography* is of the utmost importance, in order to render the Scriptures either plain or profitable.... Many persons read the Bible...without ever taking the trouble to inquire whereabout the places mentioned in it are situated. Yet there are numerous passages which have little meaning to one who does not attend to the geography; and other passages which have peculiar beauty when we have the whole position of the scene in our minds.
> *Ernest*. Please to mention one or two of these.
> *Uncle*. I will give you an example of the advantages of biblical geography. You have often read the account of the journeyings of the Israelites....
> *Hilary*. Yes, and they were forty years making the journey....etc., etc.[22]

The author of *Uncle Austin and His Nephews*, James Waddell Alexander (1804–1859), a Presbyterian minister and professor at the Princeton Theological Seminary, published many other religious and socially-concerned works. Uncle Austin's nephews and

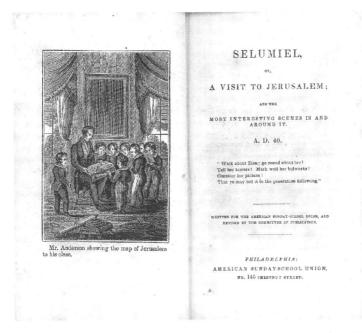

Frontispiece and title page: (Gregg), *Selumiel, or, A Visit to Jerusalem* (1833)

Alexander, *Uncle Austin and His Nephews* (1838)

" Here comes old Peter Parley once more! "

Goodrich, *Peter Parley's Tales About Asia* (1830)

Mr. Anderson's Sunday school pupils, are serious, docile, invariably "good" little boys whose only purpose in their fictional lives is to serve as a means for inculcating the A.S.S.U.'s didactic material and Christian moral principles to their real-life counterparts.

Much livelier, if less religiously-inspired, series of highly popular children's pedagogic booklets are "Peter Parley's" geographical stories, by the Connecticut-born Bostonian, Samuel Griswold Goodrich (1793–1860), who for some years served as the American consul in Paris. One of these, *Peter Parley's Tales About Asia* (1830), devotes several pages to the adventures of a shipwrecked American sailor named James Jenkins in Arabia, Persia, Turkey, Syria, and Palestine. Back in Boston, Jenkins relates his story to his old friend Peter Parley, who had been his comrade-in-arms at the battle of Bunker Hill. At the end of this chapter, Peter Parley (Goodrich) challenges his youthful readers' (supposedly) newly-acquired knowledge by posing three questions: "Where is Mount Sinai? Where is the land of Uz? What of Arabia?"[23] In the three

blance to the French, and are as fond of amusements as the people of Paris.

From Teheran the travellers proceeded to the Caspian sea. This they crossed and entered Independent Tartary. This country they found thinly inhabited by different tribes of Tartars. Along the Caspian sea it was tolerably fertile, but in the interior it was desolate, and mountainous. They were several times attacked by the people, who seem to be given to robbery.

They soon left this inhospitable country, recrossed the Caspian sea, and entered the Caucasian countries. Here they had occasion to admire the fine forms of the men, and the beauty of the women. They now entered Turkey and visited Aleppo.

From this place they proceeded to Jerusalem. In this celebrated city they remained a long time. It is now much smaller, and far less splendid, than it was in the time of Solomon. It is about two and a half miles in circuit.

What can you tell of Independent Tartary?

JERUSALEM.

Goodrich, *Peter Parley's Tales About Asia* (1830)

decades from 1827 to 1860, the little 32mo books comprising over one-hundred titles in "Peter Parley's Method of Telling about Geography to Children," were also pirated in England by several publishers, and in all sold some eight million(!) copies.[24]

The "Peter Parley" booklets are generally acknowledged to represent a milestone in the introduction of realism to English-language juvenile literature as a whole.[25] (As Goodrich put it, his books were written to entertain and "feed the young minds upon things wholesome and pure instead of things monstrous, false, and pestilent.") In the evolution of children's books touching on the Holy Land, Goodrich's Peter Parley volume on Asia marks a new departure from religiously- and morally-inspired writing. As in his other geographical works, the presentation is purely secular and factual, with rudimentary fictional elements intended to arouse interest and a modicum of excitement in the development of the narrative.

Exploration and travel adventure fiction

Wrapping the pedagogic aims of obviously didactic, generally dull literary constructions in more attractive fictional plots was but a short step. The combination of religious and general educational objectives that permeate almost all of this juvenile literature throughout the 19th century appear already in what seem to be the first of children's adventure books based on the reports of explorers and travelers in Bible lands. In Mrs. Hofland's *Alfred Campbell, or the Young Pilgrim*, and its sequel, *The Young Pilgrim, or Alfred Campbell's Return to the East...&c.&c.*, initially published in London in 1825 and 1826, respectively, the author's dedication to William, third son of the Reverend Gilbert Beresford, epitomizes the approach:

> My Dear Young Friend,
>
> I have great pleasure in dedicating to you, this and the preceding volume of Alfred Campbell's Travels, because you manifest an ardent desire for improvement, and are at an age when the mind, unburthened by other cares, may imbibe the most happy (because pious and moral) impressions, and commit to memory with good effect every species of knowledge. You will perceive, from the perusal of these pages, that nothing of itself valuable is achieved without labour, and enter on the increasing toils of your own education, I hope in the same disposition that my young traveller exhibits, with a resolute heart and manly mind, assured that, whether *his* fatigues were recompensed or not, your own certainly will be so. The sense of conquering difficulties is itself a reward to a noble spirit, and the acquisition of knowledge is that of the best treasure man can possess on earth next to piety, which it resembles....[26]

In Hofland's first Alfred Campbell book the hero is a fourteen year-old Scottish lad from Perthshire whose mother had just died. His father, a member of the landed gentry, proposes that they travel abroad to take their minds off the tragedy:

> "Indeed! Where would you wish to go, Alfred?"
> "To the Holy Land, dear father; to the places consecrated in our hearts by the most sacred associations; to Jerusalem...which was

ENGRAVED BY E.FINDEN

Barbara Hofland (1770–1844)

once the most glorious city upon the face of the earth.... Oh! how I do long to walk on the Mount of Olives, where my Saviour has so often walked with his disciples...."

Mr. Campbell pointed out the hazards of such a trip, but Alfred, who greatly admired the hardihood of his Highland countrymen, was ready for any challenge.[27]

Barbara Hofland (1770–1844) née Wreaks, of Sheffield, and widowed shortly after marrying a Mr. Hoole, was a somewhat lackluster poet and a former Harrogate school-mistress. Her second husband, Thomas Hofland, was a talented but financially not very successful landscape painter. Under the impetus of economic

25

need Barbara Hofland became a prolific writer of books for children and youngsters. Finely attuned to the wants of the market,[28]
she produced over sixty such works, initially published by John
Harris in London, and many of them also translated into other
European languages. More than 300,000 copies were sold in England alone, and the American editions were published in large
numbers as well, making the author a wealthy woman. In her
"Alfred Campbell" books set in Bible lands (as in others) Barbara
Hofland openly acknowledges her sources:

> The Writer of the following Tour has endeavoured to present, in a
> form acceptable to Youth, the leading facts, and most interesting
> descriptions of the places spoken of, as given by approved authors;
> for which purpose she has diligently read all the latest and best
> publications.[29]

Her narrative relies heavily on William Rae Wilson's Travels in
Egypt and the Holy Land,[30] published two years earlier, and on

> ...an admirable work written by Capt. Mangles R.N.;...printed for
> private distribution only; but which she [Mrs. Hofland] is per-
> suaded the gallant author would be willing to communicate (so
> far as she has intruded upon it) to the young and inquiring minds,
> for whose information this work [*Alfred Campbell*] is compiled, and
> to whom she is anxious to present only the most authentic details.
> From the most original and interesting part of his Travels she has
> conscientiously abstained; but should she be so fortunate as here-
> after to procure his personal permission for that purpose, it is prob-
> able that her young friends may find Alfred travelling again by the
> Dead Sea and Arabia Petraea.[31]

Captain Mangles consented, and Hofland's follow-up volume, *The
Young Pilgrim, or Alfred Campbell's Return to the East, etc.*, appeared
the following year (in 1826):

> The Compiler of Alfred Campbell's Pilgrimage, being encouraged
> by its great success, [is] honoured by the permission of Captain
> Mangles to extract from his excellent and unique work, descrip-
> tions...which could not fail to inform and interest her young read-
> ers....[32]

Now, Alfred, having returned from the Holy Land six years previously and upon completion of his university studies at Cambridge, undertakes an extended trip through the eastern Mediterranean regions in the company of his friend Clayfield.

James Mangles, together with another Royal Navy officer, Charles Irby, had privately published the record of their travels in 1817-18 which included the region around the southern end of the Dead Sea—an important milestone in Palestine exploration—and a visit to Petra. Earlier in the century, in 1806-7, Ulrich Jasper Seetzen had been among the first Western travelers to leave the beaten pilgrim routes of the Holy Land and to penetrate forbidden regions of "Eastern Palestine"—the Hauran and Transjordan—and the Negev. Johannes Ludwig Burckhardt explored northern Syria, and in 1812 rediscovered the legendary rock-hewn city of Petra in the mountains of Edom. In 1816, James Silk Buckingham traveled through Transjordan and Mesopotamia. Each had to assume Bedouin disguise when venturing into these remote parts of the Ottoman empire for the "advancement of science." These men, and a few others, pioneered the modern geographical and archeological exploration of the Middle East by the West at considerable personal risk: Burckhardt died in Egypt as a result of the hardships he had endured in Arabia; Seetzen was poisoned by Bedouin; and Buckingham's life was threatened more than once. The publication of their detailed reports, diaries, maps, and sketches, which had often been drawn up surreptitiously under dangerous circumstances, sparked the imagination of their contemporaries.[33] In these accounts the element of exciting adventure and dangers was real enough. Barbara Hofland drew upon and intertwined this material and the published reports of other well-known, contemporary travelers such as Edward Clarke (1801), François de Chateaubriand (1806), William Rae Wilson (1819), and Frederick Henniker (1820-1822)[34] in her tale of Alfred Campbell's perilous peregrinations in the "East."

Closely following such authors' itineraries, Hofland's narrative takes her heroes through Greece, Turkey, Cyprus, Syria, Lebanon, Egypt, Sinai, Palestine, and Transjordan. Like the actual travelers

Hofland, *The Young Pilgrim* (1828)

and explorers, they are hospitably received along the way by fellow-Christians in Greek-Orthodox and Franciscan convents, and are helped, advised, and hosted by English consuls. Thus, in a merging of fact and fiction, Alfred and Clayfield set out from the St. Savior Monastery in Jerusalem for excursions to Jericho and the Dead Sea—despite the (authentic) attack and severe wounding of Sir Frederick Henniker there by Bedouin in 1820.[35] Brushing off the apprehensions and warnings of the anxious monks, they make preparations for visiting the recently rediscovered ruins of long-sought Petra. Wearing Arab dress, they journey to Bethlehem and Hebron:

> The Turks of Hebron having little intercourse with Europeans, are very jealous of them; and they [the two young travelers] could not, by any effort, gain admission to the Mosque, which is said to be the tomb of Abraham.... The town of Hebron is populous, but not large; the streets are winding, and the houses unusually high....
>
> They had been favourably received by the Sheikh, who entertained them with rice, milk and coffee...but threw many difficulties in the way [of their proceeding to Kerek, Wadi Moussa and Petra]. In consequence...Alfred applied to a Jewish priest, whom he thought a likely person to assist in the search for conductors. They found him in a house remarkable for its neatness and cleanliness, and learnt that he was at the head of about a hundred families of Jews resident in Hebron.[36]

The chief rabbi of Hebron indeed helped them obtain the services of a local chieftain from Kerak [Sheikh Yousouf] to guide them to their destination. But it was not the end of their difficulties. The following passage tells of Alfred Campbell and Clayfield's tribulations in visiting Petra:

> All the Wadi Moussa people in the camp joined in their chief's hostility...exclaiming, "Let the dogs go and perish if they please!" and swearing "they should neither drink of their water, nor pass into their territory." ...Old Sheikh Yousouf's [their Bedouin guide] resolution was shaken, and he tried to persuade our young travellers to give up the attempt of proceeding further; but as their curiosity was rather excited than satisfied by what they had seen, and

they were now so near the great object of their search, it will be readily supposed that they combated his suggestions....

"Now for Petra! the city of the Desert, the land of wonders!" cried Alfred, as he leapt from his hard couch at sun-rise....[37]

Having absolved herself from the sin of plagiarism by obtaining the authors' permission to use their works, the enterprising Mrs. Hofland brazenly proceeded to reproduce entire passages verbatim, without so much as paraphrasing, and only shortening the narrative and substituting her young heroes' names for those of the actual travelers.[38] Thus, the events and personages she mentions, the Arab garb of the fictitious young heroes, the places they visit, and their intrepid behavior against all odds did have a basis in truth. Within a few years, Barbara Hofland's narrative of Alfred Campbell and Clayfield's exploits was also published in Boston by Munroe & Francis and by Orville A. Roorbach in New York and Charleston, and even appeared in a freely translated German edition.[39] The last London edition seems to be that of 1853. One of her first published children's books (in 1821), that deals with the First Crusade and is also partly set in the Middle East and Palestine, is discussed below, under "Boy Crusaders."

To the extent that juvenile books on the Holy Land can be taken as a distinct category of Palestiniana literature, the importance of Barbara Hofland's Alfred Campbell stories cannot be underestimated. She is still very much the moral pedagogue, her style tends to be artless, her characters stiff and unconvincing, and the plots give the impression of having been slap-dashed together in a hurry (with an eye on much-needed royalties?) from the published source material she used so freely. But her subject matter, while decidedly "promoting Christian knowledge," has also undoubted entertainment value. Most copies of her small books I have seen are well-worn, and many have childish inscriptions and scribbles in pencil on the front and end pages, attesting long use and frequent reading; the small, engraved illustrations are often hand-colored—obviously by children. Where the original, detailed works of the travelers and explorers she drew upon were published in expensive volumes unlikely to be accessible to many families, her

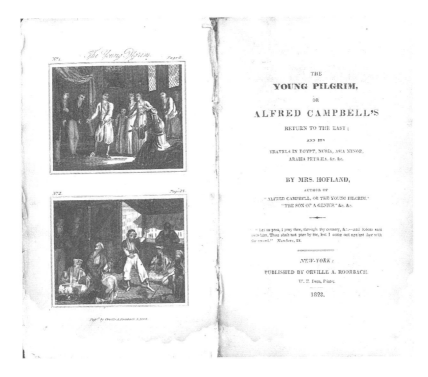

Frontispiece and title page: Hofland, *The Young Pilgrim* (1828)

children's compilations brought recent, tantalizing discoveries in Bible lands and their geography into the homes of a much larger public.

A more fantastic, sentimental example of such tendentious if informative writing is a little book apparently first published in London in 1839 (and again in 1847), *The Travels and Adventures of Charles Durand, Showing the Manners and the Customs of the Eastern Nations*, that combines an improbable adventure story in Bible lands with manifestations of exemplary religious faith. The author, Annie Peploe Molyneux (1805–1880), wrote other books for children under the name of Mrs. J.B. Webb (or, Webb-Peploe), among them the far better-known *Naomi; or, The Last Days of*

Jerusalem which is discussed below, under "Fictionalized historical plots."

The hero of Peploe's story, twelve-year old Charles Durand, is the eldest son of an officer serving in India, a "...fine manly boy, the delight of his father and mother for his obedience and affectionate disposition, whose sisters doted on him, always kind and ready to do anything in his power to please them." His greatest pleasure is reading the Bible.[40] Charles's parents decide to send him and his little sister, Emily, to their clergyman uncle in England for their education and health, and bid them a tearful farewell as, in the care of a fellow officer, they sail from the port of Calcutta. The voyage proves disastrous: Their sailing vessel is wrecked in a storm, and only Charles (with his Bible and box of tools), Emily, and a family servant are washed ashore on an island, where Emily soon dies. Charles is captured and sold into slavery to Arabs in Mocha, and resold to an Abyssinian Christian physician who takes him to Ethiopia. The boy endears himself to his kind master by his industry and ingenuity, even saving him from a vicious hyena by shooting the animal. He is redeemed by Greek monks who attempt to convert him to the Orthodox faith, but free him eventually. In the company of one of the monks whom he befriends, young Charles Durand travels through Sinai to Jerusalem, staying on the way with wild Bedouin, meeting with many exciting adventures, and overcoming dangers with resourcefulness, tact, and courage. In Palestine, where he remains for some time wearing Arab dress and visiting the sacred sites, the young hero meets Captain Munro, a British officer who is acquainted with his father. This gentleman helps him return to Calcutta by way of Asia Minor and Persia—to the supreme happiness and thankfulness to God, of Charles's family who had given him up for dead together with his sister.

One of the incidents in the narrative illustrates the author's pedagogic method. Driven by boyish curiosity and relying on his native garb, Charles had tried to enter the Temple Mount, which, as a Christian, he knew to be an offense liable to the severest punishment. Having seen him previously in the company of Greek monks, a Turkish guard challenges him:

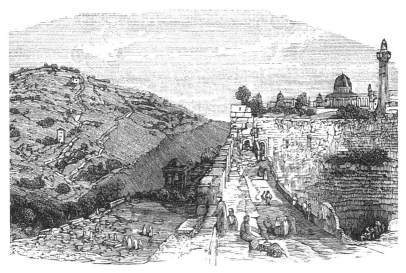

TEMPLE AREA AND MOUNT OF OLIVES.

Eddy, *Van Wert's Travels in Asia and Africa* (1884)

"Are you not a Christian?" Charles was silent for a moment. He was alarmed at the fierce, angry manner of the Turk…

"No I am not a follower of your prophet but a disciple of Jesus Christ; and I will never deny Him who died for me."

Charles Durand would not lie even when faced with certain death by torture! Providentially, he is saved by the intercession of some influential Muslims who are broad-minded enough to admire and respect his courage and high principle.[41] In narrating her young hero's adventures, Annie Peploe, like Barbara Hofland before her, developed her unlikely plots from the published travel accounts of explorers in Eastern lands.

The *Alfred Campbell* books (1825–1853), *The Travels and Adventures of Charles Durand* (1839?, 1847), and later, a similarly far-fetched work inspired by the explorations of the sources of the White Nile in the 1860s, *The Young Nile Voyagers* (1868) by Anne

Bowman were written by women, mainly for boys. The authors' vivid imagination and faculty for assimilating actual experiences of others in their stories make up for their lack of personal acquaintance with the countries they wrote about. To emphasize their

THE START TO TRAVEL THROUGH THE DESERT.   P. 53

Bowman, *The Young Nile Voyagers* (1868)

religious, moral, and pedagogic objectives they freely endow their fictitious characters, as the case might require, with even greater courage and commendable qualities than their real-life models (who, for all we know, may not always have been paragons of virtue), or exaggerate the dastardly behavior of those who wish their heroes ill. But all these more-or-less contrived plots end on a happy note. Thus, Barbara Hofland:

> We now take leave of Alfred and his friend, persuaded that every one of our young readers will be enabled, in idea, to follow them to their own homes, and conceive what the pleasure would be of meeting dear parents, friends, brothers, and sisters, after an absence so long, and frequently so dangerous....and, more especially, how fervently they thanked the God who had so safely conducted them through a land evidently suffering under His displeasure, and stript of all the glories and privileges it once so eminently possessed!
>
> We conclude with presuming to hope that those, whose hearts can so partake the emotions of our young travellers, will also remember their adventures, and find amusement in recalling to mind whatever most impressed them in this description of places and persons: as it is the anxious wish of the author to increase their knowledge in every way which can add to their innocent pleasures, and render them wise and good.[42]

Unflinching rectitude, resolution in the face of discouragement, holding parents and companions to standards of pious faith and righteousness verging on sanctimoniousness on the part of their young heroes established these as role-models for the children who read about them. Expressions of levity, innocent childish naughtiness, or happy mischief of any sort were unthinkable to the authors—and, at the time, probably to their reading public as well. The humorless, fictitious young travelers were inevitably good—very, very good. What "amusement" and excitement the authors saw fit to allow their readers never came at the expense of "elevating the moral feelings" or instructing the young mind. As one perceptive authority on the children's literature of the period remarked: "Adventure was not to be let loose without a license."[43]

And we must, of course, make allowance for ideas of what was entertaining and interesting to children conditioned by religious upbringing and Sunday-school instruction.

As will be seen below, it is remarkable how persistent such ingenuous writing on the Holy Land and religion-related subjects proved (and kept on selling!) even long after fashions in juvenile literature became overwhelmingly secular and entertainment-oriented. Although the old moralizing approach is still to be found alongside the new trends in the 1890s (as in *The Land Where Jesus Christ Lived* by Hester Douglas, published by Thomas Nelson in London and Edinburgh), it was probably so to a lesser extent in Britain than in the United States where this sort of writing can be traced well into the 1920s (e.g., Helen Patten Hanson's *A Travel Book for Juniors* to the Holy Land in the Abingdon Religious Education Texts series). On the whole, though, the tide of unsmiling didactic and moral writing for children began to recede already in the third decade of the 19th century under the masterful impact of Walter Scott's, James Fenimore Cooper's, and similar romances which, while not specifically written for children, became quickly part of their reading. The publication of Edward Lear's *Book of Nonsense* in the early Victorian years (1841) marked the acceptance of a new taste for "amusement"—in the sense that we understand the word today—in what was deemed suitable for young minds. As will be seen, this becomes apparent in the books surveyed here as well. Lear (1812–1888), by the way, who was an accomplished illustrator and artist and a close friend of William Holman Hunt, visited and worked in Palestine in 1857 and again in 1869–70 painting fine panoramic landscapes of Jerusalem.

As in all children's literature, illustrations are an important component in these works. The books are usually enlivened by specially-made wood or copper engravings and lithographs, sometimes hand-tinted. In the later works, most of the pictures are copies pirated over and over again from previously published views in the general travel literature of the countries described.

*

In the fourth decade of the 19th century the more tolerant policies toward Westerners by the Egyptian rulers of Palestine and Syria, and thereafter of the Ottoman authorities, prompted growing numbers of travelers to visit these countries and to record their experiences and observations. This new geographical material began to surface in text and reference books on biblical subjects including "sacred geography," written specially for children and teenagers, mainly for use in Sunday schools.[44] A notable example, *A Dictionary of the Holy Bible for the Use of Schools and Young Persons,* by Edward Robinson, D.D. (1794–1863), was published in Boston in 1833, and went into several editions. In compiling his Bible dictionary, Robinson, who taught at the Andover Theological Seminary, drew upon his exhaustive study of the historical, geographic, and travel literature on the lands of the Bible that had appeared until his time. It was the first book by the man who, as a result of his subsequent travels and careful observations in 1838 and 1852, gained wide recognition in Europe and America as one of the key figures in the modern, systematic exploration of Palestine.

From the mid-19th into the 20th century

By the mid-century, as Western influence increased in the Ottoman Levant, scholarly exploration, archeological discoveries, and new historical writing on the region reached unprecedented heights. Thousands of books, articles, maps, learned (and not so learned) papers on different aspects of ancient and modern Palestine and the surrounding lands of the Bible appeared in print.[45] These both stimulated and responded to a seemingly insatiable interest in the places connected with the three monotheistic religions. In the second half of the 19th century were founded the British Palestine Exploration Fund, the Deutscher Palästinaverein, the American Palestine Exploration Society, and kindred scholarly bodies which engaged in systematized study of the country and published the fruits of their research in scholarly periodicals and books.

The changes and modernization processes that occurred in the second half of the 19th century in the Ottoman Middle East, and in Palestine and Jerusalem in particular, have been described and analyzed in many published studies. The period saw the appearance of a multiplicity of missionary establishments, archeological and cartographic survey expeditions, foreign consular representations, and agricultural and urban settlement initiatives by Western religious groups—both Christian and Jewish. The first Zionist colonies were founded toward the end of the century. Although the general improvement in public security, health, and education hardly affected much of the impoverished native population, the landscapes of Palestine gradually began to take on new features: roads were paved; telegraph lines stretched across the countryside; wheeled vehicles came into use; new buildings were constructed; agriculture was developed; and, by the end of 1892, a railway connected Jaffa with Jerusalem.

It was mainly due to the new wealth created by the industrial revolution and the consequent popularization and vulgarization of world travel, that the countries of the "East"—and the Bible lands in particular—attracted ever-increasing numbers of tourists. Tourism and mass-pilgrimages gave rise to a plethora of service agencies, hotels, tour organizers, and businesses catering to this traffic, which in turn spurred the modernization of the facilities available in the country. At one point, in 1880, the Thomas Cook Company also organized and successfully conducted a special tour for young people sixteen to twenty-one years-old "on the track of the Israelites" from Egypt through Sinai to Palestine, "accompanied by a gentleman...versed in Biblical history, and capable of imparting his knowledge to those under his care."[46]

Among the tourists were many clergymen whose trips to the Holy Land were usually paid for by affluent middle-class church congregations. Traveling in the saddle, hectored by native dragomans, importuned for baksheesh, and camping out in tents, many of them felt bound to impart their experiences to the public at large—even if it meant adding yet another hackneyed travelogue to the myriad existing ones. To enliven a repetitious account of the ordinary tourist routes, a few of these authors exaggerated the dangers—real or imagined—from "wild Bedouin" robbers and "fanatical Muslims," particularly during the usual excursion to Jericho, the Jordan, and the Dead Sea, and along the rough road through the Samaria Mountains. This was ready fare to be incorporated into books for impressionable youngsters. Mark Twain, who visited the region in 1867, made it a point to ridicule such tales;[47] and Robert Morris (see below) who traveled through the country about a year after Mark Twain wrote in the same vein:

> It is unfortunate…that nearly all published communications concerning the Holy Land are from the pens of *the clergy*. These gentlemen, unaccustomed to physical hardships, give pictures colored with the hues drawn from their own fancies, rather than the facts. In comparing my own experiences with those of the Reverend this and the Reverend that, whose books fill my shelves, I marvel to see how different they have been. The enormous "fatigues" of which they speak so lamentably…were simply those of men who probably never mounted a horse before. These "dangers of travel" are simply *bosh*. The "noisy contests" of the natives are only the clamors in their own unmusical tongue for *baksheesh*, which it only needs a sharp and stern denial to stop, and to rid one's self of the pack at a word…. No wonder that the tourist hears the jackal scream at midnight, and sees "blood and thunder" upon the countenance of every Arab he meets.[48]

But, in effect, attacks by Bedouin and Muslim villagers on Europeans were reported by some of the explorers and travelers, and a number of such authenticated cases were recorded throughout the Ottoman period.[49] One such incident in particular captivated the imagination even of straitlaced gentlemen and ladies: Once, in the mid-1840s, at the Fountain of Elisha near Jericho, two Englishmen who had distanced themselves from their companions were reportedly divested of *all* their clothing and possessions by Bedouin. Loath in this state to rejoin their party, which included ladies, they succeeded somehow in appealing to their despoilers' sense of basic propriety and human compassion: one of them was allowed to keep his hat, and the other his spectacles…[50]

39

ELISHA'S FOUNTAIN.

Eddy, *Van Wert's Travels in Asia and Africa* (1884)

Scripture lands visited and depicted

Inspired by the much-enhanced opportunities for travel and the rapidly burgeoning, well-advertised tourist traffic in Egypt, Palestine, Syria, and other countries of the Levant, dozens of works for children and teenagers set at least partly in the Holy Land were published from the mid-century on. In their general presentation and the ground they covered, such books are not much different from the contemporary books for adults on the same subjects—the more so since a number of authors adapted their published material for the general reading public to creating special books for youngsters.[51] But in addition to entertaining and instructing, such juvenile books also aimed at fostering religious devotion and desirable Christian moral behavior in their young readers. They bear titles such as *The Little Pilgrims in the Holy Land* (1861), *Youthful Explorers in Bible Lands* (1870), *Boy Travelers in Arabia* (1885), *Young Folks in Bible Lands* (1892), *Things Seen in Palestine* (1913), *Twin Travelers in the Holy Land* (1919), and *A Travel Book for Juniors* (1921–1930). Individual volumes in popular, illustrated juvenile travelogue series—"Walter's Tour in the East" (1863–65), "A Family

40

Flight" (1882), "The Boy Travellers" (1883), "Van Wert's Travels" (1884), "Zigzag Journeys" (1886), "Ned Harwood's Travels" (1888), and "Three Vassar Girls" (1892)—are set in Egypt, Palestine, and Syria (more on these, below).

All of these books capitalized on the popularity of organized tourism. The standard plot follows a party of young people—in this case, on a trip to Egypt and the Holy Land—making a story of their experiences and dutifully mentioning all the sites and incidents met with along the usual tourist itineraries. Occasionally, details of costs, means of transport, health precautions, accommodations, and other bits of practical information ("If any of Our Young Folks should travel in Palestine, inquire in Beyrout for Joseph Sharra, and it will be a happy thing if you can place yourself under his charge.") are worked in as part of the narrative.[52] The groups sometimes consist of entire families, or of several youngsters having diverse interests and led by knowledgeable mentors—distinguished relatives, teachers, clergymen. Rules of conduct drawn up for the trip are great favorites:

First.—We must begin every day with singing a hymn, Bible reading and prayer. We are to read the whole Bible *through* while in Bible countries.
Second.—We are never to speak unfriendly to each other.
Third.—Our diary *must* be made up *every day*, unless we are sick.
Fourth.—We are *never* to travel Sunday.
Fifth.— If any hard thoughts toward each other arise in our minds, they are *always* to be forgiven and forgotten, before we go to sleep.[53]

In emphasizing the more general appeal of their books, many of the authors take for granted their clients' concern for an appropriate religious approach. The Baptist preacher, the Rev. Daniel C. Eddy (1823-1896) is typical in assuring readers (or rather, their parents or adult relatives) of his "Walter's Tour in the East" series that "Moral teaching has been blended with geography and history," and that "Such incidents will be recited and such facts presented, as will interest and instruct boys and girls, and give even adult minds some idea of the romantic East, the aim of the author [being] to impart permanent benefit, as well as to amuse and please the reader."[54] Nor is proverbial matter-of-fact Yankee business sense ever far removed from Eddy's writing. Thus, for example, in Jerusalem, when visiting the site of the Potter's Field—Haceldama, the Field of Blood—bought, as related in Matthew 27:3-8, with the wages of Judas's treachery, the tragic theological association of this spot stirs his young hero to inquire:

> "How much, father," Walter asked, "are thirty pieces of silver, the price of Christ's betrayal?"
> "Thirty silver *staters*, each of which was worth about three shillings English money."
> "Let me see how much that was:...so the price paid must have been about four pounds and ten shillings."
> "Yes, my son, that was the price at which your Lord was sold. A slave in Carolina will sell for a thousand dollars, but the Lord of life and glory was traded away for less than twenty-five dollars."[55]

The last three decades of the 19th century and the fifteen years before the First World War were a time of growing influence and physical penetration of the imperialist powers in the Middle East—especially after England gained financial control of the Suez Canal in 1875. The American author of *Zigzag Journeys in the Levant: Vacation Rambles from the Nile to the Holy Land* (1886), who was much impressed by the British occupation of Egypt in 1882, prefaces his book with the declaration that besides purporting "to amuse and entertain" his young readers, he intends to

> ...interest young people in history and heroic records, and especially in the *present* political history of the countries to which the journeys are supposed to be made. Young people should be made intelligent about the politics of other lands. The writer has endeavored to give, in this volume, as clear a view as possible of the present aspects of the Eastern question, and of the governments of the countries of the Levant; so that when a young reader of the book shall see telegrams from the East in regard to political movements, he may better understand them, and be able to follow current history as it shall be recorded by the telegraph.[56]

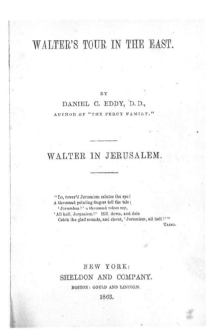

WALTER'S TOUR IN THE EAST.

BY
DANIEL C. EDDY, D. D.,
AUTHOR OF "THE PERCY FAMILY."

WALTER IN JERUSALEM.

" Lo, tower'd Jerusalem salutes the eye !
A thousand pointing fingers tell the tale ;
' Jerusalem ! ' a thousand voices cry,
' All hail, Jerusalem ! ' Hill, down, and dale
Catch the glad sounds, and shout, ' Jerusalem, all hail ! ' "
TASSO.

NEW YORK:
SHELDON AND COMPANY.
BOSTON: GOULD AND LINCOLN.
1863.

Frontispiece and title page: Eddy, *Walter in Jerusalem* (1863)

The public apparently thought well of such children's travel books. Press reviews of Edward and Susan Hale's "A Family Flight" series praised them as some "of the best books of instruction for bright young folks...." The authors, whose "names...are guarantee of high literary merit, ...allowed the children in *Family Flight*, through questions which brought pleasant stories and pertinent explanations, to make an attractive book."[57] But B.W. Johnson, the author of *Young Folks in Bible Lands* (1892), does not entirely concur—justifying his own, less popular, work with perhaps a touch of envy at the Hales' success:

> ...Amid the vast mass of literature prepared for Christian young people we do not find a satisfactory account of that portion of the world which has been hallowed forever by the feet of our Lord, his Apostles and other chosen men of God. I do not forget the well-

CAPTAIN PARKER AND MEMBERS OF THE NORTH-END
HISTORY CLUB IN EGYPT

Frontispiece: Stratton, *Our Jolly Trip Around the World* (1903)

written "Family Journey" of E.E. Hale, but one who reads it for information concerning the East is disappointed. The description of the countries visited is subordinate to the story, and when one has finished it he has much more vivid impressions of the adventures of the "Horners" and "Stuyvesants" than of Egypt and Palestine. Yet any work that will serve to interest Young Folks in Bible Lands is a gain.[58]

Echoing a contemporary fashion of global travel,[59] around the turn of the century there appeared several books on trips around the world by groups or classes of school children, under the tutelage of teachers and other responsible adults. *A Run Around the World* (1891), *A Journey Round the World* (1901), *Our Jolly Trip Around the World with Captain Parker* (1902), all include visits to the Holy Land and Egypt.

The travelogue serials

The earliest travelogue-type children's books on the Holy Land were probably Henry S. Osborn's *The Little Pilgrims in the Holy Land*, and the six-volume series of Daniel C. Eddy's "Walter's Tour in the East" (*Walter in Egypt*; *Walter in Jerusalem*; *Walter in Samaria*; *Walter in Damascus*; *Walter in Constantinople*; and *Walter in Athens*)—published at the time of the American Civil War (1861–1865). Both these American clergymen had themselves visited the Middle East and produced books of their travels upon which they drew in constructing their semi-fictitious stories for youngsters.[60] A closer look at the American juvenile travelogue storybook series of the 1880s and 1890s places those volumes dealing with the countries of the Middle East in a more universal context.

In view of the commercial successes of books on visits to different countries, and of contemporary literary works of travel adventure by authors such as Herman Melville, Mark Twain, and Jules Verne, editors of publishing houses also commissioned travel writing for children. Among the men and women who took up these challenges were editors of children's periodicals and contributors to these—writers experienced in producing juvenile literature. In

45

Book cover: Butterworth, *Zigzag Journeys in the Levant* (1886)

one case, Harper's requested Henry M. Stanley, the famous Africa explorer, to prepare a condensed version for "young folks" of his two-volume *Through the Dark Continent*. Stanley, who disclaimed having any "experience in juvenile writing," nor time to devote to this, turned to the author of the widely-read "Boy Travellers" series, Col. Knox, with the suggestion that he make it into a volume on Central Africa.

With such books selling between several hundred thousand to over a million copies of each series, travel writing for children was indeed a profitable enterprise. It was acclaimed by parents and educators as an effective alternative to lifeless, didactic school texts; and children apparently read these books with interest. Well-advertised new accretions to these series in attractively bound quarto volumes were usually placed on the market just before Christmas, each new instalment being eagerly awaited. One devotee reminiscing from her childhood told of "a series of Christmas trees, growing taller as I grew, and in the pile of presents a copy of Hezekiah Butterworth's *Zigzag Journeys in Europe* or one of its successors...always I asked for it and got it."[61] Not all of these children's travelogue series included volumes on Middle Eastern countries, and so the present survey does not cover the "Rollo," "Bodley," and "Knockabout Club" books, nor several other current series of this genre.

It was the popular "Zigzag Journeys" series that firmly established the new style. The idea was not original but a development of French children's books on travel by vacationing schoolboys and their teacher in Switzerland and other countries, *Voyages en zigzag* by Rodolphe Toepffer. The American series was started at the instigation of the Boston publishers Dana & Estes in 1880 by Hezekiah Butterworth (1839–1905), a well-known Bostonian writer and editor of a highly successful children's periodical, the *Youth's Companion*. A lifelong bachelor, Butterworth, was portrayed by a contemporary as "strongly religious, completely unsophisticated, and conscious always of moral responsibility."[62] His early stories about small children—"little Emily" and "little Willy"—usually depicted them as "so good that they died young." Butterworth's interests ranged from poetry to folklore, from history to contemporary politics, and he was also influenced by the long tradition of Goodrich's "Peter Parley" tales. His "Zigzag Journeys" are a mishmash of fact, fiction, folktales, Christian hymns, morsels of ancient history, and geographical notices presented in the form of (bewildering) digressions from the narration of the travels of a pair of youngsters and their adult mentor. The characters are different for each journey in a given part of the world. By 1895 Butterworth had produced seventeen volumes of "Zigzag Journeys." The seventh book in the series, published in 1886, was *Zigzag Journeys in the Levant, with a Talmudist Story-Teller. A Spring Trip of the Zigzag Club Through Egypt and the Holy Land*, which is appropriately seasoned with pious religious readings and biblical references.

To cash in on this profitable literature, the hardly less prolific Mrs. Elizabeth Williams ("Lizzie") Champney (1850–1922) launched her "Three Vassar Girls" series in 1884, aimed at twelve-to sixteen-year old girls. The author grew up in a puritan home in Deerfield, Massachusetts, opened out to the world during her student days at Vassar, married a well-known New York artist, was on friendly terms with Walt Whitman and John Greenleaf Whittier, and later during a prolonged residence in Paris and England, also with John Ruskin and Dante Gabriel Rosetti.[63] Her publishers, Estes & Lauriat of Boston, exerted continuous pressure for an annual addition to the series—whether or not she happened to be personally acquainted with the countries through which she took her young heroines. The writing is therefore uneven in terms of geographic and historical accuracy, and is loaded with fairly predictable melodrama and contrived situations. But Lizzie Champney had a liberal, broad-minded outlook and often introduced themes showing up common prejudices. The last of the eleven volumes of her "Three Vassar Girls," *Three Vassar Girls in the Holy Land*, published in 1892, addresses common manifestations of anti-semitism as part of the story (see below, under "Prejudices and conceptualizations—Jews").

The most reliable and thoroughly researched of the juvenile travelogue writing in the latter two decades of the 19th century

Book cover: Champney, *Three Vassar Girls in the Holy Land* (1892)

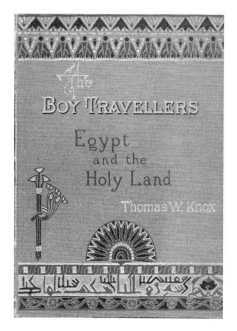

Book cover: Knox, *The Boy Travellers, Egypt and the Holy Land* (1882)

Book cover: Hale & Hale, *A Family Flight over Egypt and Syria* (1882)

50

are the "Boy Travellers" books by Thomas W. Knox (1835–1896). Knox, who had served in the Civil War as a Lieutenant-Colonel in the Union army, was among the most renowned American travelers in his time, "roughing it" in some of the most remote, wild regions of the world. From early youth in New Hampshire he had dreamt of traveling, with a special interest in the Holy Land. He later worked as a newspaper reporter and wrote many books for adults and boys based on his extensive experiences in many countries. Knox's "Boy Travellers" series was started somewhat unassumingly in 1879 with *The Boy Travellers in the Far East*, and spread into "nearer" parts of the "East" and Africa over the following four years. Thus, *Part Fourth: Adventures of Two Youths in a Journey to Egypt and the Holy Land* appeared in 1882; the series ended with the fifteenth volume in 1894—*Boy Travellers in the Levant. Adventures of Two Youths in a Journey through Morocco, Algeria, Tunis, Greece and Turkey, with Visits to the Islands of Rhodes and Cyprus, and the Site of Ancient Troy*. Knox, who had first-hand knowledge of each of the regions he describes, takes his three heroes, Frank Basset and Fred Bronson, and their all-knowing mentor, Dr. Bronson, through all of them. These characters constitute the only fictional component in his books; for the rest, half of his compositions are original writing, and the others compilations taken from reliable sources. As will be seen below, Knox was endowed with a sense of fairness and respect for other peoples, even those commonly regarded as "savages" by his contemporaries, and took pains to inculcate this in his young readers. Contemporary assessments of the series varied from "stodgy and dull" to "bubbling over with fun, fact, and fiction." On the whole, the too-solidly-packed "Boy Travellers" were probably rather less popular than Butterworth's "Zigzag Journeys."

The "Family Flight" series of travelogue books by the well-known Boston Unitarian clergyman, the Rev. Edward Everett Hale (1822–1909) and his not less notable younger sister, Susan Hale (1833–1910), round out the list of the most popular of such works published in the 1880s. The second volume of the five in the series, *A Family Flight over Egypt and Syria* (1882) is based on the actual experiences of the authors in the Holy Land, but with much of the factual background material drawn from various published guidebooks and other popular texts. Of the four contemporaneous series, the "Family Flight" books are the best in terms of the quality of writing—mainly Susan Hale's. The lively if rather inane plots are constructed around the chatty, leisurely progress of the fictional Horner and Stuyvesant families along the well-worn tourist routes in Egypt and Palestine. These works aim more at facile entertainment than at imparting "useful knowledge," on the assumption that the young can gain more from actual travel than from books. The characterization of the Hales' young heroes is more imaginative than in the preceding series: the two adolescent

Susan Hale (1833–1910) and Edward Hale (1822–1909)

Horner children focus on art and history, while the younger boy notices small details and strange peculiarities in the countries visited. In the light of the earlier work of Robert Morris discussed below, that appeared about a decade previously, it seems not unlikely that the Hales borrowed the idea from him, or were at least inspired by it.

All of these attractive quarto travelogue volumes published from the 1870s on are profusely illustrated, almost entirely in black-and-white but with an occasional colored lithograph frontispiece. Most of the pictures are steel engravings of original drawings, engravings after photographs, and photographic plates. The publishers, Estes & Lauriat in Boston and Harper's in New York, allowed unlimited use of their extensive pictorial archives to the authors. The same illustrations therefore appear and reappear in the various volumes. However, some of the writers or their family members were talented artists or amateurs in their own right. They added their sketches and drawings to the existing resources to help visualize the settings and heroes of the narratives.[64]

Surprisingly, I have not found any juvenile travelogue books of this genre, and more specifically on Scripture lands, in Britain— except perhaps for Tilt's *The Boat and the Caravan* (see under "A family tour in Egypt and Palestine," below). Nor have I come across evidence for these books being sold in England. I have no satisfactory explanation why this should have been mainly an American phenomenon of the last decades of the 19th century, when very many travel books in Bible lands for adults were published in England. Nor do I know whether similar books were produced in other European countries at the time.

The Nile and Pyramids, drawn by Susan Hale

Hale & Hale, *Family Flight over Egypt and Syria* (1882)

Robert Morris (1818–1888)

Robert Morris — the youthful explorer

If to single out one book that best exemplifies all of the foregoing, but has an added attribute—a sense of humor—that is conspicuously lacking in almost all the others, the choice must fall on *Youthful Explorers in Bible Lands* (1870, and later editions in 1871 and 1874) by Robert Morris. A lawyer by profession and former Masonic Grand Master from La Grange, Kentucky, Morris (1818–1888) was a prolific writer, poet, and lecturer on Freemasonry, and a committed Protestant. In 1868, he undertook a study trip in Europe and Palestine with funds provided by Masonic lodges throughout the United States, and as a result produced an interesting book, *Freemasonry in the Holy Land*,[65] which saw several editions. Well-read in Palestine travel literature and history, and knowing his Bible intimately, Morris rode and walked through the country with only minimal recourse to local tourist guides. His personal charm and great sense of fun enabled him to make easy human contacts. And he was nobody's fool. His notes and observations are crisp and incisive, and contain important information

54

on contemporary personalities and events in Palestine, among them, on the "Adams Colony" in Jaffa.[66]

Along with the preparation of his travel book, the enterprising Morris wrote a book for youngsters:

> To make the numerous facts applicable to the Holy Land interesting to the young, it is found necessary to resort to pleasing fiction. We adopt that of a party of pious, well-instructed children, traveling in Bible countries, under the guidance of a gentleman experienced in Oriental researches...
>
> Elliot (12), John (17) and Harriet Morrell (20), are the only children of Mr. Ebenezer Morrell, a wealthy and pious merchant of New York.... He put them under charge of Mr. Richard Fountain, Superintendent of the Sunday School of which Elliot, John and Harriet are members.... Their three diaries make up this book.
>
> *Such is our simple fiction.* In its use we will give our readers fresh and abounding information upon the Scenery, Ruins, Productions, Customs, Antiquities, and Traditions of Scriptural countries, written in styles adapted to all classes of readers, and in a variety such as has never before been attempted in a book upon this subject.[67]

And indeed, the *Youthful Explorers* is chock-full of observations, background information, and all sorts of interest-holding digressions, many—but by no means all—taken from the author's *Freemasonry in the Holy Land*. Each chapter is arranged in the form of four diaries, starting with Elliot's boyish notes, through John and Harriet's progressively more serious descriptions, and ending with a few judicious remarks by Mr. Fountain as the guide and mentor of his three charges. Robert Morris was a writer of considerable ability, for he manages to be convincing in each of the four roles by adopting a different style appropriate to each diary. His boyish ebullience and his eye for revealing detail come to light mainly through Elliot's diary, as in the following random examples:

> The Arabs say there are three hundred and sixty uses for the palm tree, one for every day of the year. I can name a three hundred and sixty first—*it is good for boys to climb*. I name this palm tree [at Lydda] Judas Maccabæus, for we are now coming into the district where that great warrior and patriot won his immortal fame.

55

He is one of my nine heroes and I know his history by heart...and carved his initials, "J.M.," on it, with my knife.[68]

...I was surprised to see a kerosene lamp [in an Arab house], just like ours at home...Mr. Fountain told me that...there were three ship loads of kerosene sent to this country from the United States last year..."Hurra for Uncle Sam," I hallooed when I saw it. The man, when he heard that, answered *tyeeb* ["good"].[69]

The streets of Jerusalem to-day are full of pilgrims dressed in all sorts of costumes, and travellers who are not pilgrims, English, French, German, Americans, etc. One Yankee sea captain rolling along, full of arrack and sin, caught hold of my arm and stopped me and said, "Boy, can you tell me anything about the people of this country?" Says I, "Yes, I can." "Well, then," said he, "tell it." Said I, "they never refuse *baksheesh!*" He let me go with a laugh that could be heard to the top of Mount Olivet, and said I was right."[70]

Elliot is getting pretty sharp with these legend-mongers. They have told him so many lies, and contradicted themselves so often, that he scarcely shows patience with any of them. A Greek priest, who undertook, to-day, to point out the rock on which the cock crowed that recalled Peter to penitence, was dumbfounded by El-liot asking him if he had ever heard of Peter the Great sailing across the Dead Sea, in a lead coffin, with his head under his arm! [John's diary].[71]

And so, one chuckles through the adventures of the Youthful Explorers—but never at the expense of commendable Protestant piety, replete with all the conventional conceptions regarding be-nighted natives and "other" Christians, solid information, and the inevitable assimilation of "useful knowledge." Robert Morris in-tended this volume of the *Youthful Explorers* dealing with Jaffa and Jerusalem to be the first of six on the entire country. But the materials he had prepared were destroyed in the Chicago fire of October 1871, and although there is a record of a later edition in 1874,[72] I have not been able to ascertain if it goes beyond the original text. Nevertheless, even the first volume of Morris's in-novative writing for children on the Holy Land, which went into several editions, must have been known to the authors who began to turn out juvenile travelogue books on many countries in the subsequent two decades. One is tempted to guess that it served them as a model, although none of their somewhat hackneyed travelogue books on the Holy Land succeeds in being as fresh, enjoyable, and informative as *Youthful Explorers in Bible Lands*.

*

Today, reading through a number of the latter-19th-century travelogue books on Bible lands is dull, tedious business. The predictably repetitious "plots" of all these travel books are a function of the standard tourist itineraries followed and the sacred and historic sites visited. Only the differences in the young traveller-heroes' characters and the authors' literary ability, style, and individual outlooks provide more-or-less credible interest and entertainment. There is never any deviation from prevailing ideal standards of Protestant Christian behavior and sentiment, even if these are no longer as explicitly advocated as in the earlier works of the first half of the 19th century examined above.

Although several of the juvenile travel books on the Holy Land still blend geography and history of Scripture lands with moral teaching, from the 1860s on there is a noticeable decline of pious exhortations in favor of factual information enlivened by added elements of adventure. No longer are fantastic and improbable— not to say preposterous—plots devised in all seriousness by the authors. Matter-of-fact realism had arrived, and earlier emphasis on "goodness" had largely given way to wisdom in the practical ways of the world: how to organize and budget effective tours, holding one's own in bargaining with Orientals, securing good deals and advantages, "handling" natives, taking health precautions, acquiring souvenirs, discounting superstitious monkish tales about holy places, keeping a diary, and the like.

Where, as has been seen, the early, exciting discoveries in Bible lands in the first decades of the 19th century found their way into children's books on the Holy Land, much of the subsequent archeological research and exploration was often far too technical and scholarly to stir the imagination of the average reader. Modern systematic archeological excavation only came into its own around the turn of the 20th century, and popular writing on the new discoveries dates mainly from the mid-20th century on—after the period under discussion here. What relevant, new information materialized from the intensified research in the latter half of the 19th century, was crystallized and integrated in the excellent, popular pocket-size guide-books—Murray's, Baedeker's, Cook's, and the like—without which no self-respecting tourist would think of venturing into Egypt and Palestine-Syria—and any other foreign country, for that matter. Much of the practical advice and route descriptions woven by the authors into the structured stories for youngsters of travels through Bible lands can be traced directly to the standard guide-books of the period.

Thus, the "Preliminary Remarks" by the knowledgeable author of Murray's two-volume *Handbook for Travellers in Syria and Palestine*, one of the earliest of these vademecums initially published in London in 1858, set the tone for such subsequent works through the turn of the 20th century and into World War I:

> I shall...introduce the tourist to the country [Palestine] he intends to visit. I shall give a short sketch of its geography and physical features, referring to phenomena which make this land one of the most remarkable in the world. I shall glance rapidly at its civil and sacred history, recalling events unparalleled for their interest, and influence on the destinies of mankind.... I shall endeavour to explain the religious creeds, and illustrate the manners and customs, of the several sects and races that now inhabit the country. I shall also note the nature of the climate; the disease peculiar to certain localities, against which travellers must carefully guard; and the proper seasons for visiting, with a due regard to health and comfort, the various districts. My remarks on these topics must of necessity be brief and very general; but I shall endeavour to make them so full as to prepare the ordinary traveller for viewing with pleasure and safety, and profit the scenes of Holy Writ....

The erudite author of Murray's *Handbook*, the Reverend J.L. Porter (1823–1889), who traveled widely through Bible lands and produced a number of other books on his travels and studies, went on to apprise and admonish the tourist, who presumably was of like mind and social outlook:

> ...the best specimens of humanity are here found among the lower classes. The farther we go from the contaminated atmosphere of government offices, the more successful shall we be in our search after honesty, industry, and genuine patriarchal hospitality—the great, almost the only unadulterated virtue of the Arab. They are illiterate, of course, and extremely ignorant of all Frank inventions; but...there is a native dignity in their address and deportment, which will both please and astonish those who have seen the awkward vulgarity of the lower classes in some more favoured lands....
>
> ...It has been too often the practice of Englishmen to "manage" their Arab servants and muleteers by bullying and browbeating; but this is a great mistake....such conduct is beneath the dignity of an English gentleman. Unvarying courtesy, accompanied with as unvarying *firmness*, will gain the desired object far more effectually.... At the same time, any approach to undue familiarity should be immediately checked; the permission of such familiarity will be attributed by the Arab to weakness of character...of which he will not be slow to take advantage when occasion offers. To know one's place and keep it, and to know one's rights and insist on obtaining them, are all-important qualifications in Syria.... The traveller should be careful to show...by the ease and dignity of his bearing, that, while he may enjoy a *joke*, it would scarcely be safe to trifle with him....[73]

The attitudes and mindsets behind this type of advice, which underly virtually all the juvenile books examined here, are expanded upon in some detail in the concluding chapters of the present survey.

It is well here to consider the newer juvenile writing on the Holy Land against the literary perspective of its period: In 1864 *Alice's Adventures in Wonderland* had made its appearance, followed by *Through the Looking-Glass and What Alice Found There* in 1871. Lewis Carroll's gentle irreverence and intelligent sense of fun stimulated and conditioned the imagination and consciousness of millions—both adults and children. The 1860s also saw the advent in America

THE POOL OF SILOAM.

Knox, *The Boy Travellers, Egypt and the Holy Land* (1882)

and England of "dime novels" and "penny dreadfuls," with their elements of thrilling adventure fiction entirely devoid of dogmatic religious motifs. Writing for children could never again be quite what it had been earlier. We may assume therefore that the youngsters who chose to read books on religion-related subjects now displayed somewhat more sophisticated and discriminating taste.

The change in the approach of authors to their young readers is clearly manifested in a comparison of two of the travelogue-type books mentioned above. Henry S. Osborn, the author of *The Little Pilgrims in the Holy Land* was exactly contemporary with Daniel C. Eddy who produced the infinitely more popular "Walter's Tour in

60

the East" series, the first volumes of which appeared in 1863, two years after the former. Both were American clergymen and preachers born in 1823; both had visited the lands of the Bible at about the same time and published books for adults on their travels, impressions, and studies;[74] both felt impelled to cash in on the juvenile book market by taking fictitious youngsters along the standard tourist routes they themselves had covered; both their narratives are largely constructed along catechism-type question-and-answer sequences to enliven the inevitable descriptions and the religious and historical information on the sites visited. But what a difference between them! The Rev. Osborn's "Little Pilgrims," Amy, Ettie, Rose, Sallie, Mary, and Willie, with Fannie, their young governess and teacher, touring the Holy Land in the care of Dr. and Mrs. Stewart, are of the same pious goody-goody ilk as the children in the didactic and early travel-adventure books of the 1820s and 1830s reviewed above. Here is a typical exchange between thirteen-year-old Sallie and the all-knowing Dr. Stewart:

> "Oh, how many places of interest we might speak of here! But from what you [Dr. Stewart] say, the stream of Siloam's brook is just at the foot of Mount Zion."
> "Yes, just east of it; and there too is another fountain."
> "Then that illustrates that beautiful piece of Milton's poetry:—
>
> > 'Thee, Zion, and the flowery brooks beneath,
> > That wash'd thy hallow'd feet, and warbling flow,
> > Nightly I visit.'
>
> Oh, how I shall delight to see those pleasant streams from those fountains!" etc., etc.[75]

Not that Osborn did not give early warning of what was to come in the Preface to his little book:

To The Youth Who Shall Read This Book.
My Dear Young Friends:—
I have written with a desire to improve as well as to please you. You will, therefore, have to work a little, as well as play; but if you read until you have completed the book, you will not only know

61

more of the pleasures and trials, the joys and disappointments, which attend upon a journey through that country of which the Bible speaks, but you will know more of the cities and ruins, and understand better what you have read and have been taught in the Scriptures....[76]

Not quite so, the Rev. Daniel Eddy, who seems to have been an enterprising and active personality of a more modern stamp, with a twinkle of merriment in his eye. The characters in Eddy's books: Walter, his sister Minnie, and his schoolmate Harry, travel through the Eastern Mediterranean countries with the former's parents, Mr. and Mrs. Percy of Cambridge, Massachusetts, ciceroned by their

HAGGI.

Hale & Hale, *A Family Flight over Egypt and Syria* (1882)

Egyptian dragoman Hajji Mohammed Achmet. The routes they follow in Palestine, Lebanon, and Syria are essentially the same, if in a different order, as those covered by Osborn's heroes—and by most of the youngsters in such travel books of the subsequent decades. Unlike the exemplary "Little Pilgrims," Eddy's young travelers are vivacious and full of boyish eagerness. Harry doesn't care much for serious things and does not know his Bible very well, while Alfred is of more thoughtful disposition. Poor Minnie, to her regret, has to leave the camping party through Palestine at Jaffa to accompany her ailing mother to Beirut, and Mr. Percy and the boys are joined in their travels by a number of American gentlemen. Although all the important places are duly visited and explained at some length, the story flows smoothly and makes good reading, with a neat touch of tongue-in-cheek waggery. For example, the party is

Eddy, *Walter in Jerusalem* (1863)

LEAVING SEBUSTE.

Eddy, *Walter in Samaria* (1864)

about to break their camp at Nablus, not far from the poor dwell-
ings of the meek, submissive Samaritan community:

> "Gentlemans must be done breakfast, very quick," cried [the
> dragoman] Mohammed Achmet, advancing.
> "What is the hurry?" asked Mr. Dunnallen.
> "The Samaritans will come upon us if we stay much longer."
> "Nonsense!"
> "Mr. Dunnallen, I am Mohammed Achmet, and I say the Sa-
> maritans will come."
> "Well, let them come."
> "They take my mules; they take my tents; they take my beds;
> they take my gentlemans; and they—they—they—"
> "They what?"
> "They cut my neck right off."
> "Are you afraid of them?"
> "Yes; they no good. They not Mussulmans."
> "The sun is getting high, the day is growing hot, and we have a
> long ride before us. That is what makes Hajji Mohammed in such a
> hurry to get away."
> It was not long before they were ready to start, tents pitched,
> baggage all secured, boys mounted, gentlemen impatient, steeds
> prancing and pawing the ground, and the dragoman shouting—
> "Forward!—ahead,—what you call him?—Go along!"....[77]

The Rev. Daniel C. Eddy's "Walter's Tour in the East" books went
into several editions and can still be found today (in one of my
"Walter" booklets a childish hand wrote in pencil: "this is a verry
verry good book"); the Rev. Henry S. Osborn's colorless *The Little
Pilgrims in the Holy Land* is exceedingly rare. Eddy followed up his
success in juvenile writing with new popular travel books for
youngsters, partly on the same Mediterranean regions: *Rip van
Winkle's Travels in Asia and Africa by Rupert van Wert* (1882), *Van
Wert's Travels in Asia and Africa* (1884), and *Young Folks' Travels in
Asia and Africa* (1890).

All the subsequent American travelogue books on Bible lands
seem to be more-or-less conditioned by Eddy's style and literary
constructions. But despite a freer approach to human nature, and
to children in particular, and occasional humorous and gently

mocking passages, these are always kept within clear limits this side of reverence. In all of this juvenile literature on the Holy Land there is an absolute absence of skepticism—let alone derision—regarding Protestant Christian religious and moral values, such as was voiced at that time by Mark Twain, for example, on going through the same regions:

> I am sure, from the tenor of the books I have read, that many who have visited this land in years gone by, were Presbyterians, and came seeking evidences in support of their particular creed; they found a Presbyterian Palestine, and they had made up their minds to find no other, though possibly they did not know it, being blinded by their zeal. Others were Baptists, seeking evidences and a Baptist Palestine. Others were Catholics, Methodists, Episcopalian, seeking evidences endorsing their several creeds, and a Catholic, a Methodist, an Episcopalian Palestine. Honest as these men's intentions may have been, they were full of partialities and prejudices, they entered the country with their verdicts already prepared....[78]

The popularity of the travelogue books subsided around the turn of the 20th century, presumably because they were still too obviously didactic.[79] At least in this literature dealing with the Middle East, this genre gave way increasingly to more exciting historical adventure fiction, and, for younger readers, to storybooks focussing on the lives of children in these countries and their folklore.

AN ARAB GUARD IN PALESTINE.

Knox, *The Boy Travellers, Egypt and the Holy Land* (1882)

Books for younger children

I should like to rise and go
Where the golden apples grow;—
…Where in sunshine reaching out
Eastern cities, miles about,
Are with mosque and minaret
Among sandy gardens set,
And the rich goods from near and far
Hang for sale in the bazaar;—
…Where among the desert sands
Some deserted city stands.
…There I'll come when I'm a man
With a camel caravan;
…And in a corner find the toys
Of the old Egyptian boys.

(Robert Louis Stevenson, "Travel," *A Child's Garden of Verses, 1885*)

From the 1860s on there appeared in America a number of small books for six to ten-year-olds—some of them specifically for girls—on life-styles of children in different countries, including Middle-Eastern lands, among them: *The Seven Little Sisters Who Live on the Round Ball That Floats in the Air* (1861, and until 1924), *Each and All* (1877, 1888), *Little Folks of Other Lands* (1882), *Two Little Travellers* (1883), and *The Bubbling Teapot, A Wonder Story* (1886 and 1893, by Lizzie Champney, the author of the "Three Vassar Girls" series). These were followed after the turn of the century by *Little Folks of Many Lands* (1904) and by the highly popular "Little Cousin" series written by several different authors and published by L.C. Page of Boston, among them *Our Little Turkish Cousin* (1904), *Our Little Jewish Cousin* (1904, 1925) which tells about Esther and Solomon, two Jewish children in the Old City of Jerusalem, *Our Little Arabian Cousin* (1907), *Our Little Armenian Cousin* (1907?), and *Our Little Egyptian Cousin* (1908). In those years, Black of London produced their beautifully color-illustrated series, three volumes of which are *The Holy Land*, *Egypt*, and *Turkey*. A similar work is Adela Goodrich-Freer's small-format, instructive *Things Seen in Palestine* (1913, 1927); she was one of the few authors who knew the country and its people intimately through long residence in Jerusalem.[80]

67

An assessment in the *Detroit News-Tribune* of the "Little Cousin" books considered them

> The most delightful and interesting accounts possible of child-life in other lands, filled with quaint sayings, doings, and adventures.... Juveniles will get a whole world of pleasure out of [them].... [The] pleasing narratives give pictures of the little folk in the far-away lands in their duties and pleasures, showing their odd ways of playing, studying, their queer homes, clothes and playthings.... The style of the stories is all that can be desired for entertainment, the authors describing things in a very real and delightful fashion.[81]

What all these books for younger children have in common is their focus on everyday life and on children, rather than on the physical geography and travel in the countries described. They reflect a growing desire to foster better understanding of other human beings. In this sense the authors, most of them women, make a positive contribution to the development of a more broad-minded approach to those who are different from their young American and English readers. But even here, intimations of superiority over the "native" peoples and stereotypical characterizations are never entirely absent:

> In the villages south of Damascus...the crowd is sure to contain several smiling negroes, some of them branded on the cheeks; Circassians with sickle-shaped nose...with an untamable expression on their bitter faces; Arabs, darker of complexion and more languid of eye; and Turkish soldiers, thin and small-pox bitten. Here are to be found the Jew, sneering complacently at the inferior world; the fanatical Moslem, who will break the water-bottle your [infidel] lips have touched; the Druse...to whom you hesitate to say "Good-morning"...; and the cross-bred ruffian, who has no scruples about anything.... But to what race do the mass of dwellers in Palestine belong...?[82]

(*We*, of course, are well-bred, of pure "race," proper appearance, and good character; our homes are not "queer," and our ways of playing are not "odd.") And so Aunt Hetty remarks to little Willie

Book cover: Wade, *Our Little Jewish Cousin* (1904)

Zwemer & Zwemer,
Zigzag Journeys in the Camel Country
(1911)

ARAB BOY IN A CROCKERY SHOP.

Zwemer & Zwemer, *Topsy-Turvy Land*
(1902)

Chaplin & Humphrey, *Little Folks of Other Lands* (1882)

when telling him about the native people of the Holy Land (1890):
"You see, dear, how very thankful we ought to be that we are more
enlightened...."[83]

Of more sympathetic temper regarding the native people are
several well-written, informative books for young children on Arabia by Amy and Samuel Zwemer: *Topsy Turvy Land; Arabia Pictured for Children* (1902), *Zigzag Journeys in the Camel Country*
(1911), and others. The perceptive first-hand insights of the
authors, who served as missionaries in Bahrein for many years,
are however larded with purposeful indoctrination of a rather
treacly sort. The Zwemers end almost every chapter on aspects
of Arab and Bedouin life in their books with exhortations to their
youthful readers to help the poor "blind" Muslims whose "religion
is false":

> ...Oh how crooked is the way of God which Mohammed taught in
> his book! Sadder still, what a crooked way it is that the Moslems
> walk!... Do you not think God wants *you* to carry the gospel to
> them and send them teachers to learn the way of Jesus?
>
> We tell you all this about them that you may pray for them that
> God may soon send more missionaries to preach these precious
> words. We want you all by prayer and offerings to help put a silver
> lining in the dark clouds of their lives.[84]

As one American educator wrote two World Wars later: "Ideas are
given to young readers most easily—prejudices planted or eradi-
cated—so easily in fact that a grave responsibility is put upon the
writer."[85] (This facet of children's books on the Holy Land is discussed in greater detail in the final chapters of the present survey.)

A far more balanced picture of Bedouin children in Arabia, *Our
Little Friends of the Arabian Desert. Adi and Hamda*, is presented a
generation later (in 1934) in one of a series of supplementary readers for elementary school children by Frances Carpenter, and
beautifully illustrated by Curtiss Sprague. The author, an American Fellow of the Royal Geographical Society, makes it a point to
state in her Preface that her heroes are not depicted as "curiosities
or 'funny foreigners,' but as living men, women, and children with

the same basic needs as our own," and that "the idea of world friendship and interdependence underlies the plan of the series" on children of different lands. The story is very well written and thoroughly researched, not in the least due to the guidance Carpenter received from Alois Musil, the famed Czech authority on Bedouin life. It is therefore the more disconcerting to present-day sensibilities to read that "Adi and Hamda are as brown as our American Indians. With such dark skins it seems strange that they really belong to the White Race, as we[!] do. But their features are very like those of American children...."[86] And the Black male and female slaves in the Bedouin's households are mentioned as a matter of course and elicit no comments by the fair-minded author.

A small volume purporting to interest and inform younger children about the Holy Land is Hester Douglas's *The Land Where Jesus Christ Lived* (1890). Even though very few late-19th- and early-20th-century texts for children are still as artlessly tendentious, convoluted, and tightly-packed with amalgams of biblical-historical and eschatological Christian ideas, such concepts were never far removed from the consciousness of most writers. Consider, for example:

"...How is it that their [the Jews'] land has so many different names?...."
"...It is called the Promised Land because, hundreds of years before the Israelites entered it, indeed long before there were any Israelites at all, God promised their forfathers, Abraham, Isaac, and Jacob, that he would give it to their descendants.... When, at last, Joshua led them into it, they found it peopled by heathen tribes, who were descended from Canaan, the youngest son of Ham, one of the three sons of Noah; and it was from [them]...that it received the name of the Land of Canaan. When the Israelites conquered and lived in it, it got the name of the Land of Israel. It was called Palestine after the Philistines...whom the Israelites never drove out. And it is called the Holy Land because all that is most sacred in the world's history is connected with it. It is not only the land that God picked out from all the countries on the face of the earth to give to his own chosen people...but it is the land in

which Jesus Christ, the Holy One, was born, and in which he lived, and died, and rose again...."

"Yes, thank you, auntie; I must try to remember about all these names. Which of them all do you like the best...?"

"I scarcely know, Willie,...but I know which I like the least—Palestine.... It sounds too heathenish.... I never liked to think that a heathen race, however brave or powerful, should have given their name to the land in which God's people lived.... If the Israelites had only trusted in God and faithfully served him, they would soon have driven out the Philistines, as they drove out the other heathen races that they found occupying the land; and then this heathen name would never have been given to the country. The name of Palestine seems to me nothing but a reproach."

"And do you like Canaan, auntie? I suppose not, for that was a heathenish name too, you know."

"Yes, I like Canaan, and very much too, heathenish as it may appear.... It tells of a land taken by faith and by hard fighting out of the hands of heathen possessors.... If we, who are God's true Israelites, fight in his name and strength, we shall assuredly conquer and take possession of the land promised to us as the Israelites did...and then we shall have a Land of Israel of our own.... The name of Canaan spurs us on, as Christian soldiers, to nobler action.... The bright Canaan towards which we are journeying will soon be all our own, and we shall live in it. It denotes *possession*. And the Holy Land—that is a beautiful name!.... There sin will reign no more; and where there is no sin there will be no sorrow.... But the name of Palestine, my boy, has nothing to do with that dear and blessed land; for none but God's own faithful people will ever enter it...."[87]

What mental picture of the Holy Land could little Willie possibly form from such outpourings? Where did "useful Christian knowledge" end and rapturous theological metaphor begin? Were "stories" of this kind and style really read to (or by?) small children—still in the 1900s? If indeed, at the time, in some of these books younger children were being subjected to the tenacious old moral, pietist, didactic conventions, their elder brothers and sisters were engrossed in exciting adventure and travel books.

THE HEAD OF THE CARAVAN.

[*Page* 37.

(Strauss), *Helon of Alexandria* (ca. 1865)

II.

FICTIONALIZED HISTORICAL PLOTS

A DISTINCT category of juvenile literature on the Holy Land is that of works based on dramatized biblical or historical episodes in which imaginary young heroes play exciting roles, or in which biblical or historical personages are presented in fictitious situations—but at least in reasonably plausible geographical settings. Harriet Martineau (1802–1876), a Unitarian tending to positivism, dedicated abolitionist, feminist, and pioneer in the field of sociology, toured Egypt, Sinai, and Palestine in 1847, walking much of the way. In the Preface to the 1870 edition of her *Times of the Saviour and Traditions of Palestine* she explains what induced her to write this rather tiresome, if apparently appreciated, treatise:

> In my early youth it was a grand discovery to me,—as I have seen it to be to almost all the intelligent children I have known,—when I passed over from the dreamland or fairyland of the Bible to the perception that the Holy Land had a geographical place in our world, and that its cities, villages, lakes, and mountains could be visited at this day, and the journeyings of the personages of the New Testament History among them traced by the record like the travels of common men. From the time of that exhilarating discovery my interest in Jewish Archaeology, and the Geography and Natural History of the Eastern lands, was inexhaustible.

One day the thought occurred to me…to describe, with all possible fidelity, the aspect of the life and land of the Hebrews at the critical period of the full expectation of the Messiah.[88]

Early precursors of this type of writing were some of the little plays on biblical stories that were performed in girls' schools, such as *Ruth and Naomi* and *The Binding of Isaac* by the French countess Stéphanie Félicité de Genlis (1746–1830). At least one of these, *Hagar in the Desert*, was published in English translation "for the use of children" by Isaiah Thomas in Worcester, Massachusetts in 1785.[89]

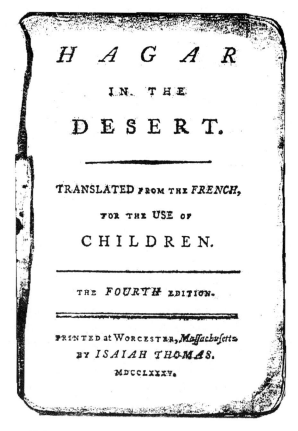

Title page: de Genlis, *Hagar in the Desert* (1785)

A few fictionalized developments on Old and New Testament themes and on the Apocryphal Books of Maccabees are included in the expanded bibliography at the end of this volume. But the main historical episodes to be repeatedly dramatized for young people in this way are the first Jewish Revolt against Rome and the destruction of the Second Temple and its aftermath in 66–73 as described by Josephus Flavius; the Crusades—particularly, the Third Crusade led by Richard I in 1189–1192; and the wars of the British in Egypt and Palestine in modern times—against Napoleon Bonaparte in 1798–1801, the occupation of Egypt in 1882, the Sudan campaigns in the 1880s and 1890s, and the First World War. In all of these, the fictitious heroes and minor characters interact with real, colorful historical figures as documented in contemporary chronicles, personal memoirs, historical writing, official histories, and later, also journalistic reportage.

In constructing their more-or-less historically plausible—not to say authentic—interest-holding plots, the authors of such works juggle recorded source material with imaginary situations, and frequently also interpolate ideological, moral, religious, and political messages. Charlotte Yonge, in the Preface to her *The Prince and the Page; a Story of the Last Crusade* (1865, and many later editions), dwells on this predicament:

> …The author is well aware that this tale has all the incorrectnesses and inconsistencies that are sure to attend a historical tale; but the dream that has been pleasant to dream may be pleasant to listen to; and there can be no doubt that, in spite of all the inevitable faults, this style of composition does tend to fix young people's interest and attention on the scenes it treats of, and to vivify the characters it describes; and if the sketch at all tends to prepare young people's minds to look with sympathy and appreciation on any of the characters of early annals, it will have done at least one work.

With this caveat let us look more closely at the different historical periods and episodes upon which this highly popular literature is built.

The Jewish War

Perhaps the earliest of the English children's books set in the time of the Jewish revolt against Rome appeared in 1826 as "Aunt Jane's" (Mrs. Christina Isobel Jane Johnstone, 1781–1857) rendering of Josephus Flavius's *The Wars of the Jews* "adapted to the capacities of young persons." The author tells us that she gave the book to her niece, Little Anne, for her birthday and traced with her the story on the map of the Holy Land.[90]

Naomi; or, The Last Days of Jerusalem, a fictionalized development based on Josephus but with the addition of extensive Christian themes, was first published in 1840 by Annie Peploe (Mrs. J.B. Webb, the author of *The Travels and Adventures of Charles Durand*, discussed above). Her writing is priggish and sentimentally cloying, and the intent is explicitly evangelical. But the tale extending over 400–odd, tightly-printed pages is nonetheless dramatic and engrossing, for she closely follows the stirring, detailed narration of Josephus—a participant and eye-witness in these momentous events. Mrs. Webb's work was later taken up by the Presbyterian Board of Publications and became so popular that by the end of the century it was reprinted many times in numerous editions, including in Finnish, Danish, German, Yiddish, and Icelandic translations, the latter as late as 1929. Some of the editions, among them a sumptuous one, are finely illustrated with reproductions of engravings and lithographs by well-known artists such as W.H. Bartlett, Sir J. Gilbert, and David Roberts who drew and painted also in Palestine. The last English edition appeared in 1899. In the preface to the original edition of *Naomi*, the author explains what impelled her to write this long and elaborate story:

> The signs of the present times point strongly towards the Holy Land and the once glorious city of Jerusalem; and the eyes of many (both Jews and Gentiles) are turned thither in anxious expectation of the approaching fulfillment of those promises of favour and restoration which are so strikingly set forth in Scripture, with reference to that land and her scattered and degraded people…and the same hand that has scattered her inhabitants over the whole

Annie Webb-Peploe (1805–1880)

earth, and made them a mark of scorn and reproach of the Gentile nations, can…gather them together and bring them again into their own land.

Believing that such considerations may be both interesting and useful to her young readers, the author has ventured (with a full sense of her own incompetence to do justice to the subject) to attempt a narrative of which the scene is chiefly laid in Jerusalem….[91]

Later, in the Preface to the revised, 17th edition of *Naomi* in 1860, Webb-Peploe reformulates her purpose in the light of messianic Christian "proto-Zionist" ideas that during the two intervening decades were gaining increasing support in English and American evangelical as well as political circles. Among the leading protagonists of the restoration of the Jews to the Land of Israel were the

NAOMI;

OR, THE

LAST DAYS OF JERUSALEM.

BY MRS. J. B. WEBB.

CHURCH OF THE HOLY SEPULCHRE, JERUSALEM.

LONDON:

W. NICHOLSON AND SONS,

26, PATERNOSTER SQUARE, E.C.,

AND ALBION WORKS, WAKEFIELD.

Title page: Webb, *Naomi; or, The Last Days of Jerusalem* (ca. 1855)

Christadelphians led by John Thomas; Col. George Gowler and the Earl of Shaftesbury, both of whom drew up specific proposals for the settlement of Jews in Palestine under British aegis; the Mormons in America; and others. She writes:

> If when this book was first written the Author could say that the "signs of the times pointed strongly towards the Holy Land and the once glorious city of Jerusalem, and that the eyes of many—both Jews and Gentiles—were turned thither in anxious expectation," how much more emphatically may the same assertion now be made!
>
> The interest felt for God's ancient people, the Jews, has been gradually increasing; and their condition as a people, has been greatly improved. Many decrees have been passed in their favour in various lands; and in few civilized countries are they now subjected to either persecution or contumely....
>
> All this...leads us to hope that...the same Almighty power which has turned the fruitful field into a "desolate wilderness," will cause that wilderness to blossom as the rose; and the same hand that once scattered the Jews over the face of the world...will "bring them again to their own land," and make them the "joy of the whole earth."
>
> The Author cannot forbear here expressing her sense of the favour and indulgence with which her attempt to portray "the last days of Jerusalem" has been hitherto received; and her earnest hope that it may have led some of her readers to feel a greater interest in the Jews, and to "pray for the peace of Jerusalem." Let us pray also for their conversion, and their preparation to meet their expected Messiah: for thus shall we be exercising the highest duties of Christian charity, and repaying in the best manner our obligation to those unto whom the promises of God were first made....

The author of *Naomi* uses the writing of Josephus as a vehicle for propagating the messianic theme of the restoration of the Jews to their ancient land as the essential precondition for the Second Coming.

In the late 1880s the same source material derived from Josephus was worked into a well-written adventure story, *For the Temple*, by George Henty, and after the turn of the 20th century,

JOHN AND HIS BAND IN SIGHT OF JERUSALEM

Henty, *For the Temple* (ca. 1888)

also by Rider Haggard, in *Pearl Maiden* (illustrated by the Pre-Raphaelite artist Byam Shaw). The prospectus for the former proclaims that:

> Few boys have failed to find the story of the revolt of the Jews of thrilling interest when once brought to their notice; but there has hitherto been little choice between sending them to books of history and supplying them with insipid fictional transcripts of the story [an obvious allusion to Webb-Peploe's *Naomi*; J.S.]. Mr. Henty supplies a distinct want in this regard, weaving into the record of Josephus an admirable and attractive plot. The troubles in the district of Tiberias, the march of the legions, the sieges of Jotapata, of Gamala, and of Jerusalem, form the impressive and carefully-studied historic setting to the figure of the lad who passes from the vineyard to the service of Josephus, becomes the leader of a guerilla band of patriots, fights bravely for the Temple, and after a brief term of slavery at Alexandria, returns to his Galilean home with the favour of Titus.

82

Solitudinem Faciunt Pacem Appellant

Haggard, *Pearl-Maiden* (1903)

Underlying the above writing for young people based on Josephus's *Jewish War* is the fundamental Christian belief that the violent end of the national independence and consequent dispersion of the Jews came as divine punishment for their rejection of Jesus as the Messiah—a theological concept that has survived to this day. This motif is also integrated in Henty's and Haggard's fictional narratives on this theme, although the purport there is far less evangelical than Webb-Peploe's and is not the primary concern of the authors, who focus and build their plots upon the exciting action of the historic events described.

Boy Crusaders

From the early 19th century on, a number of important medieval source works on the Crusades were translated, edited, and published in English in popular form, and new histories written. Among these are Mills's two-volume *History of the Crusades* (1820), Bohn's *Chronicles of the Crusades* (1848), biographies of Richard I (1855, 1857), and in the 1890s, Archer and Kingsford's *The Crusades* (1894), and several works in the Palestine Exploration Fund's "Palestine Pilgrim Text Society" series, including Beha ed-Din's *The Life of Saladin* which presents a view of the Crusades from the Muslim perspective.[92]

This is not the place to discuss the mid-19th-century fascination with medieval civilization and the romanticized neo-Gothic revival in Victorian Britain, Germany, and other European countries, as well as in the United States. Although Protestant revisionist historiography represented the motivation behind the "popish" Crusades as unholy, and questioned the morality of dispossessing the Muslims in Palestine,[93] 19th- and early 20th-century English writers of juvenile books eagerly seized upon the national, ideological, and romantic aspects of this material in constructing attractive historical adventure plots, at least partly in Holy Land settings. Notwithstanding the inherent anti-Catholicism of most of the writers, in all these works the old Catholic view of devout, heroic, chivalrous Christian dedication to the "liberation" of the Holy Sepulcher and other Christian holy sites from Muslim desecration is resuscitated and held up as an absolute, overriding ideal—right throughout World War I and thereafter. The British troops fighting the Turks in Palestine in 1917–18, were commonly seen as modern Crusaders battling the Saracens: "We call General Allenby the 'modern crusader,' for he is a strong, Christian man; he represents a powerful Christian nation, and by conquering Palestine from the Turks he brought this sacred country once more under Christian rule."[94]

The appended bibliography lists over twenty works on the Crusades for youngsters in English, among them the purely biographical *Richard the Lion Hearted* (1855) by F.L. Hawks "designed more particularly for the instruction and improvement of the young," and J. Abbott's *History of King Richard the First of England* (1857). Most are fictional treatments, such as J.G. Edgar's *The Crusades and the Crusaders* (1859, 1860, 1868) and *The Boy Crusaders: A Story of the Days of St. Louis* (1865); C.M. Yonge's *The Prince and the Page; a Story of the Last Crusade* (1866 and many subsequent editions until 1930); F.B. Harrison's *Brothers in Arms* (1885); Wm. Everard's *Sir Walter's Ward* (1888); B. Alexander's *Tales of the Saracens* (1890); G. Hollis's *A Slave of the Saracen* (ca. 1902) and *Between Two Crusades* (1908); "Stephen and Nicholas: Boy Crusaders" by K.D. Sweetser in her *Ten Boys from History* volume (1910); W.G. Stables's *For Cross or Crescent* (1927); and others. The stories deal with the aftermath of the First Crusade following the defeat of the Crusaders by Saladin at the Horns of Hattin in 1187 and his reconquest of Jerusalem, the Third Crusade in 1189–1192, the Sixth Crusade in 1228–1229, the Seventh Crusade in 1248–1254, and the Eight Crusade in 1270.

ON THEY SURGED WITH FLASHING SPEARS AND SCIMITARS

Haggard, *The Brethren* (1904)

The earliest of these works, from the prolific pen of Barbara Hofland, was *Theodore, or the Crusaders* first published in 1821 (four years before the first of her "Alfred Campbell" travel books discussed above). It appeared in numerous subsequent editions and translations on both sides of the Atlantic, the last ones as late as 1879 and 1886. In her Advertisement at the beginning of the book, Hofland states that

> It was the intention of the Author...to have written an introductory chapter, explaining the times, the terms, the mode of warfare, and other circumstances connected with the Crusades, but on reconsidering the matter, she thought it more advisable to give this very necessary information, by way of dialogue in the story itself, as more likely to engage the attention, and impress the memories of her young readers.
>
> The Author will be found to adhere faithfully to facts, and dates, in her narrative, conceiving that all works written for young people should be especially careful on these points. Theodore is of course fabulous, but she trusts not unnatural, for the times in which he lived—whatever relates to his royal Master Richard Cœur de Lion, will be found to coincide with the accounts of his character and history as given by Hume, Gibbon, and that excellent publication, Mill's History of the Crusades.

Hofland and many of the other juvenile fiction writers on this historical subject devote very little space to descriptions of the physical Holy Land (which most of them had never visited). A commonly-adopted conceit has their young teen-age hero or heroes of humble circumstances join the Crusade as the page boy(s) of one of the participating knights. The youths distinguish themselves by their courage, prowess at arms, loyalty, and resourcefulness. They are noticed by the king, and are eventually knighted ("win their spurs") even before coming of age, after chance encounters and other fortuitous happenings reveal them to be of noble blood. Usually, in those books dealing with the Third Crusade, Robin Hood and his men are also worked into the plot at some point. It is hard to establish to what extent, if any, Barbara Hofland's little volume inspired and affected subsequent writing of

Theodore introduced to King Richard.

Page 94.

Conquest of Jerusalem.   *Page 15.*

Hofland, *Theodore, or the Crusaders* (1824)

this kind. Did she invent her construction or derive it from earlier romances? There can be no question, however, of Sir Walter Scott's (1771–1832) literary impact.

Scott's *The Talisman; a Tale of the Crusades* was first published in 1825 (four years after Barbara Hofland's *Theodore*) and has appeared in innumerable editions in many languages to this day. His romantic tale, which drew in part on medieval chronicles, fired the imagination of young and old alike with the thrilling, chivalrous encounters of Richard the Lion-Heart and Saladin in the Holy Land. Scott's plot features his hero in several disguised identities: Sir Kenneth, the lone Knight of the Leopard, appears at one point as an Ethiopian slave, but is eventually revealed to be David, prince-royal of Scotland; and the Saracen warrior Sheerkohf, the "Lion of the Mountain," appears also in the guise of the wise physician El Hakim and turns out to be Sultan Saladin himself. Scott, who had never been to Palestine himself, was careful to consult published accounts of travelers:

> ...The love of travelling had pervaded all ranks, and carried the subjects of Britain into all quarters of the world.... Palestine, endeared to the imagination by...sacred remembrances had been of late surveyed by British eyes, and described by recent travellers. Had I, therefore, attempted the difficult task of substituting manners of my own invention, instead of the genuine costume of the East, almost every traveller I met who had extended his route beyond what was anciently called "The Grand Tour," had acquired right, by ocular inspection, to chastise me for my presumption. Every member of the Travellers' Club who could pretend to have thrown his shoe over Edom was, by having done so, constituted my lawful critic and corrector.[95]

Thus, for his descriptions of the Dead Sea and the Ein Gedi oasis where some of the action is set, Scott relies on his friend, John Carne, one of the more important English travelers in the early 19th century,[96] but allows romantic imagination to overdramatize reality:

...A knight of the Red-cross, who had...joined the host of the Crusaders in Palestine, was pacing slowly along the sandy deserts which lie in the vicinity of the Dead Sea...where the waves of the Jordan pour themselves into an inland sea, from which there is no discharge of waters.

The warlike pilgrim had toiled among cliffs and precipices.... Issuing from those rocky and dangerous defiles, he had entered upon that great plain, where the accursed cities provoked, in ancient days, the direct and dreadful vengeance of the Omnipotent.... Crossing himself, as he viewed the dark mass of rolling waters, in colour as in quality unlike those of every other lake, the traveller shuddered as he remembered, that beneath these sluggish waves lay the once proud cities of the plain...the land as well as the lake might be termed dead, as producing nothing having resemblance to vegetation, and even the air was entirely devoid of its ordinary winged inhabitants, deterred probably by the odour of bitumen and sulphur which the burning sun exhaled from the waters of the lake, in steaming clouds, frequently assuming the appearance of waterspouts. Masses of the slimy and sulphureous substance called naphta, which floates idly on the sluggish and sullen waves, supplied those rolling clouds with new vapours....[97]

As anyone who has been to the northwestern shores of the Dead Sea at Ein Gedi and elsewhere will agree, the silent, soothing landscape is hardly "terrifying." The deep canyons cutting through the high limestone escarpments end in broad wadis with profuse vegetation—home to many birds and animals. And waves in the Jordan, and near-waterspouts in the sea? Indeed, one contributor to an American children's magazine, who was undoubtedly familiar with *The Talisman*, writing of his own experiences at the Dead Sea concludes: "We looked for gloom and we found brightness; we had imagined turbid waters, and we found a lake exquisitely clear and delicately blue; we expected perfect silence and unbroken waste, and we found the birds singing sweetly among the tamarisks and oleanders which spring up wherever a stream finds its way from the mountains to mingle with the mysterious inland sea."[98] So much then for poetic license in geographic description.

Sir Walter Scott probably influenced many of the authors of

A tall man clothed in goat-skins sprung into the midst of the path, and seized a rein of the Saracen's bridle in either hand.

Scott, *The Talisman* (n.d. ca. 1900?)

adventure books set in Crusader Palestine. However, in marked contrast to Scott's over-romanticized history, and geographical ambiguities and errors, some of these works—notably Getrude Hollis's *Between Two Crusades* and Rider Haggard's *The Brethren*—stand out by their much more careful historical and geographical accuracy.

But it was Scott's characterization of the "Saracens" that left an indelible impact on his readers and reinforced the prevailing, deeply-ingrained, disparaging Western attitudes to Islam and Arabs. For example:

> "I well thought," answered the Crusader [to the Muslim knight—Saladin in disguise], that your blinded race had their descent from the foul fiend [Eblis, the devil], without whose aid you would never have been able to maintain this blessed land of Palestine against so many valiant soldiers of God. I speak not of thee in particular, Saracen, but generally of thy people and religion. Strange it is to me, however, not that you should have descent from the Evil One, but that you should boast of it."[99]

As many of the passages quoted in these pages show, the vivid mental pictures drawn here with so much literary skill, and the underlying presumptions of Western Christian superiority, surface time and again throughout all of the juvenile (and adult) religious, educational, and recreational English-language literature on the region. This is so even where there is a conscious attempt at representing the peoples of the Middle Eastern countries with greater objectivity, and more or less empathy and understanding is evinced toward them. Such attitudes also permeate juvenile writing on the subject in other European languages as well.

Henty and the imperialists

The unquestioned master of juvenile historical adventure fiction in his day was the Englishman George Alfred Henty (1832–1902), who turned out nearly eighty such works of considerable length in the 1880s and 1890s. (Henty boasted of being able to complete a book in twenty days.) Along with Henry Rider Haggard (1856–1925), Rudyard Kipling (1865–1936), and John Buchan (1875–1940) Henty played a key role in shaping popular attitudes to Victorian and post-Victorian British imperialism.[100] Henty's action-packed books, which were read voraciously by boys and young men—and also by girls—throughout the English-speaking world made history come alive where school lessons and textbooks were often uninspiring.[101] At the height of their immense popularity, Henty's books sold about 300,000 copies a year; by 1914 about 25 million copies(!) had been sold. Until 1891, when American editions were authorized, many of the titles were pirated in the United States. Among his war and adventure books such as *Under Drake's Flag*, *With Wolfe in Canada*, *With Clive in India*, *By Sheer Pluck: A Tale of the Ashanti War*, etc., three are set at least partly in Palestine. These are *For the Temple*, on the First Jewish Revolt against Rome; *The Boy Knight*, on the Crusade of Richard I; and *At Aboukir and Acre*, on the campaign against Napoleon Bonaparte in Egypt and Palestine in the final years of the 18th century, which marked the inception of British imperialist presence in the Middle East. (Two of Rider Haggard's historical romances—*Pearl Maiden*, on the Jewish Revolt against Rome, and *The Brethren*, on the disastrous defeat of the Crusader host at the Horns of Hattin in 1187 and the subsequent events, both published shortly after the turn of the century—were inspired by that author's visit to Palestine in 1900 and are also set in the Holy Land.[102])

Henty's young readers were impelled to identify themselves with the heroes of the exciting action "for King and Country." The tenor of his writing may be gleaned from the following passage in *At Aboukir and Acre*:

> ...He [Edgar Blagrove, the young hero of the story] ran forward and looked down.
> "By Jove!" he exclaimed, "there is a breach [in the wall of Acre] down to the bottom of the tower...a large body of French...are about to...storm the breach...!
> Leaving the tower, Edgar ran along the wall.

George Alfred Henty (1832–1902)

"Take your men to the tower at once!" he shouted to the first Turkish officer he saw. "The French are crossing the ditch."

…Edgar, burning with impatience and anxiety, led them to the breach…Some of the Turks, as the French entered the tower, had been seized with panic and fled, but a few remained at their post….

Sir Sidney Smith himself [the British commander of the defense of Acre in 1799] took his place with three or four of his officers and the handful of blue-jackets. The combat was a desperate one. The swords of the officers, the cutlasses of the sailors, the pikes of the Turks, clashed against the bayonets of the French…. Djezzar, the old pasha had hitherto taken no personal part in the conflict, but had, as was the Turkish custom, remained seated on his divan every day, receiving reports from his officers, giving audience to the soldiers who brought in the heads of enemies, and rewarding them for their valour. Now [hearing that Sir Sidney and his officers were themselves defending the breach]…he leapt to his feet, seized his sabre, and ran to the breach shouting to the soldiers to follow him…etc., etc.[103]

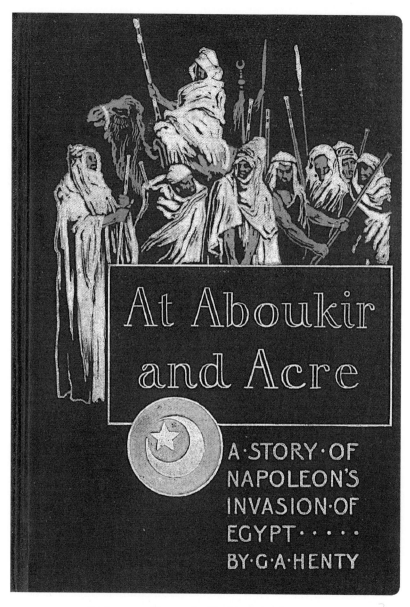

Book cover: Henty, *At Aboukir and Acre* (1898)

EDGAR THEN DELIVERED A BLOW WITH ALL HIS FORCE.

Henty, *At Aboukir and Acre* (1898)

The plot of Henty's *The Young Midshipman* unfolds around the
bombardment of Alexandria by a British naval squadron in 1882
and the beginnings of the occupation of Egypt; *The Dash for Khartoum* and *With Kitchener in the Soudan* are set in the Upper Nile and
the Sudan, in 1884 and 1898.

Henty, who had fought in the Crimean War and witnessed
violent action all over the world as a war correspondent for English papers, stresses manliness, pluck, duty to country, and readiness to shed blood when necessary to enforce authority and justice,
but also legitimate personal self-interest. He abhors milksops and
has no room for tender passion. His stock heroes are invariably
loyally patriotic sixteen- or seventeen-year-old boys who fight

95

their way to advancement and economic prosperity along well-worn, predictable plots. Bravado, disdain of "native" military prowess, and blatant White supremacy are never lacking:

> Lord Charles...said to one of the marine officers: "Captain Archer, you are to take command of that gang of fellows over there," pointing to some two hundred natives who were gathered a short distance away. "I hope we shall have a thousand at work to-morrow morning...it will be a great thing getting these gangs of natives [later also referred to as 'darkies'] at work.... Besides, they say the Egyptian troops [of Arabi Pasha] are approaching the town [Alexandria] again. I only hope they will try to come in."
>
> There was a murmur of agreement among the circle of officers....[104]

"CUTTING AND THRUSTING, THE BOYS TRIED TO MAKE THEIR WAY THROUGH."—*Frontispiece.*
Young Midshipman.

Henty, *The Young Midshipman* (ca. 1895)

HIS KEEN GLANCE SEEMED TO GREGORY TO TAKE HIM IN FROM
HEAD TO FOOT

Henty, *With Kitchener in the Soudan* (1902?)

Nevertheless, Henty does not relate to war flippantly as did some of his later imitators. After initial, light-headed enthusiasm for battle, his heroes mature as they assume leadership responsibilities and deplore wanton slaughter. Unlike in the writing of Haggard and Buchan, at least those of Henty's books surveyed here are entirely free of antisemitic remarks.

From Henty on, most of the books for youngsters set in Palestine and the Middle East fall entirely within the national-imperialist ethic, with hardly any outspoken allusion to Christian piety. Many of the British soldiers fighting in the Palestine campaigns of the First World War, who were represented in the popular press as latter-day Crusaders, must have read his and similar books.

In a similar vein, if from a parallel American perspective, is a book by Cleveland Moffett (1863–1926),[105] better known as the author of the popular Pinkerton detective thrillers. His *The Land of Mystery* (1913) also integrates actual events into the fictitious adventure story—in this case, the highly-publicized, strategically-motivated state visit of the German emperor Wilhelm II and the empress Auguste-Victoria to Turkey and Palestine in 1898. Young Harold Evans, aged sixteen, accompanied by his friend Jack McGreggor of Chicago and by a faithful old Turkish family servant, searches for his renowned medical missionary father who disappeared under mysterious circumstances. When his mother is also inexplicably abducted in Cairo, Harold and his companions contrive to discomfit sinister machinations by native Levantines in tracking down Dr. Wicklow Evans (Harold's father), and cleverly engineering his escape from the Mar Saba Monastery in the Judean Desert where he is held prisoner by a scheming Greek priest. After a succession of thrilling, cliffhanging adventures, the mysteries are resolved and the happy family reunion effected when Harold succeeds in gaining the attention of the "Great Christian Emperor, the most powerful potentate of Europe, who, with much pomp and ceremony, was making a tour of the Holy Land."[106] The magnanimous monarch, who had heard of Dr. Evans's disappearance, decisively intervenes on his behalf with the Turkish authorities. Although Moffett evinces admiration for the arrogant German emperor (who was rather less well thought-of in England at the time) it is primarily the manifestation of European imperialism that he esteems.

Where the intrepid actions of Henty's young heroes have the full force of British imperial military and naval power behind them, Moffett's Harold Evans derives his self-assurance from the prestige and moral weight of the United States. At one point, he stops the fierce "Xeibecks" about to grab him at the behest of Basil, the wicked Greek monk: Assuming a heroic stance, clenched fist on chest, Harold proclaims commandingly: "Don't touch me! I'm an American citizen!"[107]

"Don't touch me!" said Harold. "I'm an American citizen."

Moffett, *The Land of Mystery* (1913)

Harold meets the Emperor.

Moffett, *The Land of Mystery* (1913)

Moffett was a skilful writer and apparently held his readers' attention. My copy of this book has a carefully handwritten dedication to its original young owner inside the front cover: "Hoping you will get as much enjoyment from reading this story as we have, your classmates in room III."

The First World War and the Palestine Mandate

Still in the spirit of Henty's imperialist bravado are three books for youngsters romanticizing the dramatic events of World War I in the Middle East: *The Wonder of War in the Holy Land* (1919) by Francis Rolt-Wheeler, Lt.-Col. Frederick Brereton's *With Allenby in Palestine* (ca. 1920), and *The Boys' Life of Colonel Lawrence* (1927) by Lowell Thomas.

Rolt-Wheeler (1876–1960) was the author of many books for boys in the popular "U.S. Service Series," "Museum Series," and "Wonder of War Series." David Surch, the teen-age hero of his war adventure story, is the son of Professor Surch, an eminent archeologist of the "American Exploration Fund" working in Mesopotamia (Iraq). With the entry of Turkey into the war, his father sends David to seek safety with a friend in Basra. The boy, who speaks Arabic and some Turkish, contrives with the help of loyal Bedouin friends, to outwit the Turkish and German military authorities and to join up with the British and Indian forces fighting their way up the Tigris toward Baghdad. Later in the story, Professor Surch advises General Allenby on the best tactics for taking Beersheba by coming up through the Negev desert and locating the necessary water sources for the British troops at Ruheibe, Khalasa, and Bir Asluj (as actually happened). Rolt-Wheeler, who has his fictitious heroes interact with imaginary and real persons in actual events, obviously relied for these details of remote sites on the then recently published accounts of explorations in the "southern desert" of Palestine (the Negev) by T.E. Lawrence and C.L. Woolley, and on the writings of the American geographer Ellsworth Huntington on that region.[108]

Surprisingly, the senior British military officer, Lt.-Col. Brereton's (1872–1957) story, *With Allenby in Palestine*, shows up the author's ignorance of the landscapes in southern Palestine where he places the action. Brereton, who produced a number of other boys' war adventure books set in other parts of the Middle East (and elsewhere), was Henty's cousin and enthusiastic emulator. But his writing is far less competent. Despite his obvious lack of personal knowledge of the country, Brereton was probably impelled to write the story at his publishers' (Blackie & Sons) urging to cash in on the great popular interest in the British campaigns in the Holy Land. Since the book appeared in 1920, long before the official British history of the "Great War" was published in 1928 and 1930, he must have drawn on preliminary official military records for the factual background to his narrative, and probably also on some of the first journalistic accounts written while the fighting was still going on.[109]

Brereton's plot is built around the adventures of a very young Scottish subaltern, Donald Carruthers, who distinguishes himself in a number of secret intelligence missions at the time of Allenby's advance toward Gaza and Beersheba from the desert borderlands of Sinai and the western Negev (and later in Jerusalem). The implausible, if exciting, narrative describes non-existent rocky outcrops, "forests," "bubbling springs," and streams of fresh water in a region that is virtually arid and generally of a flat or gently-rolling sandy-lœss topography in the southern parts of the Gaza Strip.[110] His hero, who has a smattering of (Scottish-accented?) Arabic, is much of the time disguised as a Bedouin and chats freely with local Arabs and Turks without arousing suspicion. The author's cavalier attitude to the many British killed and maimed in the fighting (not to mention the enemy's even greater casualties) as imparted to his young readers is summed up in a remark by Carruthers's commanding general:

> ...it's the price we pay! It is the price of empire.... He went off humming a tune, for if losses sometimes weighed heavily on the General he was at least philosophical, and realized that war without its thousands of casualties was an impossibility.[111]

"AS ALLAH WILLS!" HE CRIED. "EXCELLENCY, I SURRENDER"

Page 156

Brereton, *With Allenby in Palestine* (1920)

Book cover: Thomas, *The Boys' Life of Colonel Lawrence* (1927)

COLONEL LAWRENCE AND THE AUTHOR

Thomas, *The Boys' Life of Colonel Lawrence* (1927)

The American journalist Lowell Thomas's (1892–1981) *The Boys' Life of Colonel Lawrence* was first published in 1927. T.E. Lawrence's personality and reputed military genius have since been subjected to a variety of critical assessments. But deservedly or not, Lawrence left his mark on the history of the Middle East. It was Lowell Thomas's glib photographic and written reportage of Lawrence's imaginative (partly imaginary?) exploits that made him into "Lawrence of Arabia." Thomas himself gained world fame largely through his articles, books, and hundreds of slide-illustrated talks on Lawrence. His book for youngsters, in which one of the chapters is entitled "The White King of the Arabs," is an even more theatrical narrative of Lawrence's adventures from boyhood on, among them his travels as a young student in tracing the steps of "the Crusader knights of old [who] fought to liberate [Jerusalem] from the swarthy Saracens."[112] (Yet again, shades of Sir Walter Scott!)

With the British forces in Palestine widely publicized as "latter-day Crusaders," new books on the Crusades, such as Stables's *For Cross or Crescent*, were published (in 1927 and 1936), and a few of the earlier works for younger readers (e.g., Goodrich-Freer's *Things Seen in Palestine*) were reissued in amended, updated editions.

A few children's books now reflect the new British Mandatory rule in Palestine and the growth of the Jewish community in the country. It is interesting, for example, to compare the eleventh (1925) printing of Mary Hazelton Wade's (1880–1936) small-format book for young children, *Our Little Jewish Cousin*, with the pre-World War I edition that first appeared in 1904. Wade, who in another of her children's books on Palestine did not desist from antisemitic stereotypes ("Jewish noses"),[113] had initially written in the Preface of this book:

> ...They [our little Jewish cousins] cannot say of this land or of that, "It is ours," for they are homeless. Palestine, which was once theirs, is now in the hands of the Turks. Jerusalem, the city they love best in the whole world, is in the power of those who look with scorn upon the Jewish people....
>
> These Jewish cousins would say to us "Our people suffered greatly. Yet they do not lose courage. Our parents tell us stories of the glorious past, over and over again. They will not let us forget it, and they teach us to hope for the time when Jerusalem will again be ours, and a new temple, in which we shall be free to worship, will stand upon the spot where the old one was destroyed."[114]

In the 1925 edition of *Our Little Jewish Cousin*, published after the 1917 Balfour Declaration promising the Jews a "national home" in Palestine and following the establishment of the British Mandate over Palestine, Mary Wade added an updated Introduction to precede the Preface:

> From the chaos and tumult of the recent great war there emerged a glorious realization when Palestine opened its arms once more, tenderly, as a home and nation to the Jewish People.
>
> Since the days of Nebuchadnezzar, through the regime of the Persians and Macedonians, and under the cruel administration of

the Turks, the Jews have struggled bravely in an unhospitable world, praying for the day when they might again enjoy their liberty.

In 1920, Sir Herbert Samuels [sic], an orthodox Jew, well-versed in English diplomatic principles and zealous of his people's welfare, took up the government of Palestine. Under the mandatory rule of Great Britain (such as was granted at the Versailles Peace Conference to powerful nations, that they might watch over the weaker peoples that obtained freedom in the World War) we may expect the same unselfish cooperation as has characterized the attitude of England in its dealings with all nations.

The rapid progress of the Jewish protectorate in the last five years, and the interested countenance of all religions, heralds a wonderful future to our worthy cousins who have at last, after centuries of silent and courageous endurance, been given the opportunity to become a nation.[115]

One wonders at Mrs. Wade's ambivalence regarding Jews in the Holy Land and their transfiguration from rather negative characters into "our worthy cousins." Her outlook now reflects the idealized hopes in the new world order that was supposedly emerging from the bloodshed of the war, and in the liberties gained by formerly oppressed national groups—in this case, the Jewish National Home in Palestine, with all its messianic connotations.

The new idealism surfaces even in an outspoken religious education text about a young boy's tour of Palestine with his father, *A Travel Book for Juniors* (1921–1930) that enthuses about British "Christian" rule of the Holy Land. It contains passages such as "...father says that we cannot expect everyone to look at things in the same way, and if other people are dead in earnest about what they believe, we are bound to respect them even though we don't agree with them."[116] And one of the "Things [for the young reader] to Find Out" at the end of a subsequent chapter is, "Should Americans consider themselves better than people of other countries?"[117]

British rule in Palestine brought with it new settings also for children's adventure fiction. Air Commodore Lionel Charlton's (1879–1958) *Near East Adventure*, was published in the mid-

NEAR EAST
ADVENTURE

by

Air Commodore L. E. O. Charlton
C.B., C.M.G., D.S.O.

Illustrated by Ernest Ratcliff

THOMAS NELSON AND SONS L.^{TD}
LONDON EDINBURGH NEW YORK TORONTO PARIS

There was a deafening explosion.

Frontispiece and title page: Charlton, *Near East Adventure* (ca. 1935)

1930s. It is a gripping tale of two (English and Scottish) working-class boys held by drug smugglers in Syria, and their rescue by Bedouin, the Royal Air Force in Transjordan, and the Palestine Police. At the end of their tribulations, the young heroes of the story, Bob Hilton and Len McIntosh, are graciously received in Jerusalem by the High Commissioner for Palestine and his wife, and even get to ride in the official Rolls Royce. Charlton's fluent, absorbing writing is however tainted by coarse antisemitic remarks and characterizations ("...the fat, oily countenance of the Jew shopkeeper gave me a feeling of nausea,"[118] etc.). His strong dislike of Jews and patronizing attitude to servile, "good" Arabs was fairly typical of the mind-sets of many of the British officials and military men and their families pursuing careers in Palestine of the Mandate.

An American adventure book set in the Middle East in the early 1930s is William Dixon Bell's *The Sacred Scimiter* published in 1938, but written at least a year or two earlier. The story ("...of mysterious international intrigue that no boy can afford to miss"—according to the publisher's blurb) is rather silly and the quality of Bell's writing leaves much to be desired. The "flying twins," Will and Dave Hope, true innocents abroad, meet with many strange adventures in the course of their touring and sight-seeing flight around the world—in this case from Persia to Baghdad, across the desert to "Transjordania" and Arabia, and ending up in Jerusalem. Unlike the experienced Royal Air Force officer, Lionel Charlton, Bell does not seem to know much about aircraft: the twins' single-engine *Bird of the Occident* only requires "tanking-up with gas and oil" and an occasional pliers-and-wire repair job to keep going under all conditions, including violent desert simooms. In an unsophisticated way the story reflects contemporaneous American uninvolvement (isolationism?) and considerable ignorance of world affairs.

The unsuspecting Dave and Will, are hired by an Arab woman to fly her around the region on private business. In the end, the "woman" turns out to be a decidedly male British agent in disguise, and the "private business," a determined intelligence effort to thwart a Wahhabite Bedouin uprising with the covert connivance of the local "Sherifian" kings and princes against British rule in the "secret hope of Mohammed again being supreme in Jerusalem." In the story, the Arab fundamentalist Islamic nationalist characters do not "like the way the Jews crowded the Arabs away from the Wailing Wall in that city…and thought that if the Jews were allowed to go on with their Zionist movement they would finally cover Mesopotamia, and spread their obnoxious religion everywhere."

Although the text is full of stereotypical "orientalist" concepts and confused knowledge of Arab life-styles, the author of *The Sacred Scimiter* obviously took pains to "read up"—if rather uncritically and one-sidedly—on the current events in the Middle East. Thus, when the British secret agent justifies his activities to the boys by explaining that the "Arabs want an independent empire stretching from Teheran through Arabia, and Egypt, and the Soudan, to the west coast of Africa, [and] it is costing England fifty million dollars a year to keep down this war sentiment," Dave

Dust jacket: Bell, *The Sacred Scimiter* (1938)

demands aggressively, "Why doesn't England withdraw then, and let them have their country? They have a right to their own country and their liberty." Upon which the Englishman replies: "…England never draws out, she has the reputation of being a bulldog, and if you let her alone she will make this Arabian desert a pleasant and productive part of the world. All His Majesty's Government is getting out of this is an opportunity to spend money…the king will stay with it even if your Arabian friends are standing around watching for a chance to drop a match in the dry grass." But all things considered, the Americans' sympathies and identification remain with the kindred British rather than the Arabs.[119]

*

Much of the "historical" writing examined above draws on files of contemporary newspaper reportage and official war records, but also on some of the authors' extensive personal experience and knowledge of the events they describe.

Unlike Kipling's sometimes enigmatic, deeper, imperialist soul-searching, the ideal standards of empire implicit and explicit in Henty's, Haggard's, Brereton's, Buchan's, and Charlton's (and later, W.E. Johns's) writing—that were accepted as a matter of course by the American authors mentioned here—were simple and straightforward. Their youthful, daring, totally committed, patriotic, empire-oriented heroes were not jingoist politicians or clever manipulators. Many of them were sportsmanlike public school boys and enterprising, manly adolescents from the middle or working classes. Their Christian moral values were self-understood as a natural part of their national and class identity. They were secure in their racist view of mankind, in their own innate sense of White superiority over colored peoples ("…Indians, niggers, and half-breeds, the scum of the earth"). The twisted Bible-connected morality of their imperialism had been given extreme expression earlier, in a Southeast-Asian context, by Charles Kingsley (1819–1875), the author, among other works, of the Victorian juvenile classic, *The Water-Babies*:

> Did not God bless those terrible righteous judgements? Do you believe in the Old Testament? Surely, then…what does that destruction of the Canaanites mean?…. If it be wrong, then Moses, Joshua, David were wrong…. You Malays and Dayaks of Sarawak, you…are the enemies of Christ, the Prince of Peace; you…are all the more dangerous, because you have a semi-human cunning. I will, like David, "hate you with a perfect hatred, even as though you were *my* enemies." I will blast you out with grape[-shot] and rockets, "I will beat you as small as the dust before the wind."[120]

And one critic (with a Dutch name) wrote in 1908:

> There is no doubt that the immortal Henty and his hosts of imitators have made the British nation the most conceited people on this earth…. After fourteen or fifteen years' perusal of "piffle" written apparently for his own edification, the young Englishman leaves

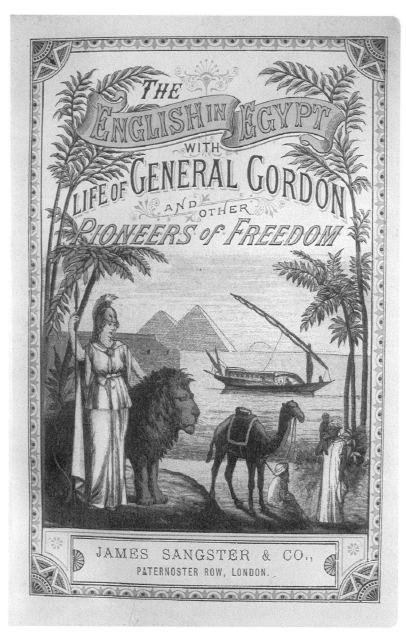

Book cover: (Anonymous) *The English in Egypt* (1886)

home and country with the very firm idea in his head that he, personally, is equal to two or more Frenchmen, about four Germans, an infinite number of Russians, and any quantity you care to mention of the remaining scum of the earth.... With the English officer class at the top of the pecking order....[121]

Thus, "...nationalism and racism, sanctioned by Old Testament Puritanism and Social Darwinism, created an atmosphere in which the normal control of the beast in man could be seriously weakened."[122] To accuse men like Henty and Haggard of such excessive views is probably too harsh a judgment, but they certainly were no innocents in this respect, and did not shrink from imparting large doses of imperialist morality and stereotypes to their impressionable young readers.

*

The historical adventure and action books produced from the 1880s into the 1930s, almost entirely devoid of overt religious content, bring well over a century of English-language juvenile literature on the Holy Land into recent history. At the end of the period under review here, there began to appear Zionism-motivated books, such as *Amnon: A Lad of Palestine* (1931) and *Pilgrims to Palestine and Other Stories* (1940), for Jewish youngsters. But children's books reflecting the new and different contexts presented by Zionist settlement efforts, Palestinian and pan-Arab nationalism, the Jewish-Arab conflict, the State of Israel, internal Arab and Jewish cultural and religious developments, regional power politics and interests, etc. are beyond the scope of the present survey.

ELISABETH ET SIONA SUR LA TERRASSE

Harry, *La petite fille de Jérusalem* (1914)

III.

FIRST-HAND IMPRESSIONS OF REAL-LIFE YOUNGSTERS AND PERSONAL MEMOIRS AS HISTORICAL SOURCE MATERIAL

CONVENTIONAL, idealized conceptualizations of the "Holy Land" were deeply ingrained. In one account the English children on board the steamer taking their family from Alexandria to Jaffa, illustrate commonly-held mental pictures:

> "...I don't think many people go to Jerusalem now, it is too far, and too difficult a journey; at least not people *we* should care for. I never heard of children going to Jerusalem since the time of the Jews."
>
> "Oh, Phœbe, you remind me of Jane; don't you remember when she was packing for us how she said she knew there was a wilderness in Jerusalem, but she did not know people could get to it? Or Dick, who said he thought Jerusalem was in the *cloods?*"
>
> At this Sylvia laughed heartily, as the two girls always did at the oddities of their father's old Scotch servant. He was one of that large class of good people who think of Jerusalem the Golden, or who will even accept Jerusalem the desolate; but Murrays's Jerusalem,—no, it is altogether repugnant to their ideas.[123]

Moreover, preconceived, largely negative attitudes regarding the native people in Scripture lands were so prevalent that very few, if any, of the authors even suspected that their own observations and impressions were colored by bias.[124]

Some of the children's books on Bible lands described above

were the work of authors who had never been to Palestine themselves. Most of these works at best reflect fleeting personal experiences in those countries, and draw extensively on travel accounts by others and on information gleaned from standard tourist guidebooks, such as Murray's, Baedeker's, and Cook's. As has been seen, in endeavors to enliven scriptural associations for their readers, some of the writers move their young heroes through exciting, fantastic adventures in biblical sites. Other, less subtle authors take youthful armchair travelers along the well-trodden tourist and pilgrim routes in artless Sunday-school teaching style ("You have more stories about the Jordan, I know, auntie. Will you tell me another today, please?" "Yes, I have more, Willie.... Here is the next:—Two men were in Jericho...etc., etc.")[125]. Occasional errors in locating sites, such as passing through the "Vale of Ascalon" on the way north from the Sinai desert to Gaza, or coming upon "Solomon's Pools" between Jerusalem and Bethlehem[126] (Ashqelon is north of Gaza; Solomon's Pools are south of Bethlehem), reveal some of the writers' confused knowledge of the "sacred geography" they profess to impart to their readers.

It is therefore interesting to examine the few books and memoirs of individual Americans and Britons, and of one young native Christian Arab boy, who themselves actually lived in the Holy Land for extended periods—especially those who were children at the time. Even if they saw things through Western Christian eyes, one might expect from such writers deeper insights into the realities of life in the country.

A family tour in Egypt and Palestine, 1846

Probably the earliest work based on actual experiences of children taken by their parents on the standard "Scripture Lands" tourist itinerary, at a time when this traffic was still in its beginning stages, is Charles Tilt's (1797–1861) popular *The Boat and the Caravan; a Family Tour Through Egypt and Syria* first published in 1847. Tilt, a devout English businessman, had recently returned from a protracted tour of Egypt and the Holy Land, together with his

SOLOMON'S POOL.

Eddy, *Van Wert's Travels in Asia and Africa* (1884)

wife, young teen-age son, and a young female servant. Even at that early date, the author felt compelled to offer an excuse in his Preface for yet another Holy Land travelogue book:

> So many books of travels in Egypt and Syria have already been published, that an addition to their number may perhaps be deemed unnecessary. The author is not aware, however, that any have been specially intended for young persons; and he has thought that a plain and unpretending account of a recent tour through these most interesting countries would not be unacceptable, and might perhaps draw their attention to works of more importance and better worthy of their perusal.

To give his narrative a little more variety he provides his young hero, Charles Dalton (Tilt's son), with a younger sister, Emily. (Coincidentally?, the youthful heroes of Annie Peploe's fictitious story described above, *The Travels and Adventures of Charles Durand*, that was published at about the same time, were also named

Charles and Emily.) Although Tilt's characters, Mr. and Mrs. Dalton, their two children, and their servant girl, Marshall, are fictitious, the travelogue avowedly follows his family's actual experiences in countries "where English children had perhaps never travelled before...(and should thereafter be able to read the Scriptures with greatly increased interest.)" He also promises at the outset that "...any profit from the sale of this work will be devoted to Missionary objects...in equal proportions to the Church Missionary Society, the London Missionary Society, the Moravian Mission, and the London City Mission."[127]

Tilt's *The Boat and the Caravan*, which may also be regarded as an English precursor of the later American juvenile travelogue books discussed above, reflects the actual conditions of travel at the time—the 1840s—before the construction of the railway and the Suez Canal in Egypt, when British passenger traffic to and from India followed the tedious Alexandria-Cairo-Suez overland route. Western travelers through Egypt and the Holy Land had to provide themselves with all necessities, from tents and bedsteads to food and water. A native dragoman had to be engaged along with men and animals for transport, a cook, and sundry attendants. The men carried arms for hunting and protection. No travel or taxing physical activity took place on Sundays, which were devoted to Christian devotions, study, and rest.

Slavery was then commonplace in the "East," and Mr. Dalton's Egyptian dragoman was intensely annoyed by his temporary master's adamant refusal to countenance his purchase of a black slave girl in Assouan—even at a bargain price. In summing up the incident, Mr. Dalton (Tilt) remarks that "Slavery appears in a much milder form in the East than...in our West India colonies, and...resembles the state of bondage...among the ancient Jews."[128]

The family's route included sailing up and down the Nile in a hired boat (flying the Union Jack) that also served for accommodations, with visits to the antiquity sites along the way. Palestine was reached after a strenuous overland journey on camel-back from Cairo through the Eastern Desert and northern Sinai to Gaza where the family had to remain under quarantine for several days.

FIRST RIDE ON A CAMEL.

Eddy, *Van Wert's Travels in Asia and Africa* (1884)

From there the usual pilgrims' and tourist itineraries were followed, with the Daltons staying at Latin or Greek Orthodox convents in those pre-hotel days in the Holy Land. In Jerusalem, they attended Anglican services at the newly-built "English Church" inside the Jaffa Gate. They made the journey to Jericho and the Dead Sea, and later proceeded to Nazareth and Tiberias through the Samaria highlands. They went on to Lebanon and sailed for home from Beirut.

Tilt's writing is labored and unimaginative, and only the occasional remark or show of enthusiasm for adventure by the very proper young Charles Dalton, and some attention to petty details of life in the East by Emily, barely acquit the author of his claim to having intended his book for "young persons." Essentially, the book varies hardly at all from the duller sort of contemporary Palestine travel literature. Nevertheless, *The Boat and the Caravan* went into at least five subsequent editions during the following decades, and was translated into German and Dutch—presumably because it was thought particularly suitable for pious children.

*

Other, later, works which were the result of long, first-hand experience under special circumstances in the region provide far more illuminating insights into the lives and activities of both native and Western children in Palestine, Egypt, and Arabia. As such, they constitute more-or-less important source material for the social history of the Middle East. Moreover, accounts of this nature tend to be more understanding and sympathetic to the people portrayed.

American youngsters in Jaffa, 1866–67

In September 1866, a group of 157 messianic Christian Americans, most of them from "Down-East" Maine, arrived at Jaffa in the bark *Nellie Chapin*. In anticipation of the Second Coming, they intended establishing a farming settlement to pave the way for the restoration of the Jews to the Land of Israel. After suffering deaths, inter-

JOPPA.

Knox, *The Boy Travellers, Egypt and the Holy Land* (1882)

nal dissent, and other difficulties, the Adams colony, named after their charismatic if alcoholic leader, disintegrated within less than a year. Except for a few families, its surviving members returned to New England.[129] In the group were children and youngsters, some of whose recollections and diaries make this poignant episode come alive today. Herbert E. Clark, one of those who remained in Palestine and later served for twenty years as the American vice-consul at Jerusalem, told of his family's arrival in the Holy Land:

> Being at the impressible age of ten and having always lived inland, the voyage made an impression which I shall never forget…We made land off the headland of Carmel on our forty-second day from Maine, and came to anchorage off Jaffa late in the afternoon. After some delay the colonists were permitted to land and camp on the shore north of the town, where they landed their cargo and discharged the ship as soon as possible. Here each family erected, for protection from the sun and night air, such shelter as

121

they could improvise. My father and a few others were able to get rooms in the outbuildings in the garden of the German Consul.

As the *Nellie Chapin* was obliged to anchor some two miles from shore, the unloading of the lumber was a difficult task. Exposed to the burning sun, in a climate entirely different from our native climate, within one month of our arrival my father and two of my brothers died of Syrian fever.[130]

And one of the older boys, Edwin R. McKenzie, of Indian River, Maine, left a unique record of their daily life as American farmers'

GARDEN OUTSIDE OF JAFFA.

Hale & Hale, *A Family Flight over Egypt and Syria* (1882)

children in the Holy Land. A few random entries from his diary, touching in their matter-of-fact tone, evoke the atmosphere:

From November 18 to December 1, 1866, we began plowing Monday noon with a new span of horses and I worked nine days and a half and have about six acres of good land belonging to the Greek convent on the north of Jaffa. Plowed, sowed and harrowed....

Wednesday, January 9, 1867.

We put up some pegs to hang our harness on and some nails, shelves and other things. We piled up our lumber and cleared up the plot. After dinner a lot of us boys went on a ride and had a good time....

Saturday, January 26, 1867.

It has been raining steady by showers all day. I have done hardly anything today for my side is so lame that I can hardly move. I kept tally for the boys that played ball and watered the horse and was well-nigh fagged out.

Sunday, January 27, 1867.

I got up late and found it a beautiful day. I washed and dressed and went to hear a Baptist preacher...of...Illinois, U.S.A. A very good sermon. Brother Adams preached afternoon and evening. Good old Indian River sermon. Velma and Carrie Wass had a good horseback ride in the afternoon. Carrie is not very good at riding....

Thursday, April 25, 1867.

We done nothing in the forenoon but in the afternoon we went up to the model farm and got a load of grass. The girls went with us. Alice, Esther, Velma, they enjoyed it hugely. We spent the evening in Captain A. Norton's. Most all the young folks were there. You can ajudge what kind of a time we had. Quite a number complained of our noise keeping them awake....

Friday, May 31, 1867.

Moving early for I wanted to see the folks off.... The steamer left about 12:00...we boys went up and dug potatoes. ...We plowed all of ours and picked them up so the Arabs would think they were dug and not come and dig them. Sad, two children died this morning, not many hours distant with the same disease which I know not...both between six and eight years old....

Thursday, July 4th, 1867.
Dull times for a fourth in Jaffa. We dragged out the day...
eating watermelons, damsons, and other fruit. Had some hens
and roosters for dinner.... Toward evening we went...to a grape
vineyard that George Tracy had rented.... Had a good time and it
was quite late when we all got home.... We danced in the evening
until all the fiddle strings gave out....

Thursday, July 25, 1867.
I loafed all day. Played on the fiddle, slept some and in the
evening we had a good swim...and fun enough.

Friday, July 26, 1867.
We...sold some things. In the afternoon we went for a walk, us
young folks. Went up to the model farm. I got some of the soil to
bring home to America.... I bid farewell to the old model farm....
(Note: You will find elsewhere my journeyings from Palestine.)[131]

Although not part of the published juvenile literature on the
Holy Land, the intimate record of the experiences of these home-
spun, young Americans sheds light on a significant chapter in the
modern economic history of Palestine—the introduction of modern
agricultural cultivation methods and equipment by idealistic
Christian and later, Jewish proto-Zionist and Zionist communal
groupings. The would-be settlers of the short-lived Adams colony
were visited, and their tribulations described, by American tourists, among them two important authors quoted in these pages:
Mark Twain and Robert Morris.

Other fundamentalist Christian groups came to settle in Palestine before and after the Adams colony, but we have only rare
indications of how their children saw life in the country so different from their native lands.

English children in Jerusalem, late 1870s

Representative of upper-class Englishmen who lived in Palestine
with their children is a little book, of the late 1870s, *Children at
Jerusalem. A Sketch of Modern Life in Syria*. The author was the
second wife of the Pre-Raphaelite artist, William Holman Hunt.

Living intermittently in Jerusalem, at one time also with his family, he painted romanticized, super-realistic scenes of landscapes with symbolic scriptural themes (*The Scapegoat*, *The Triumph of the Innocents*, and *Nazareth, Overlooking the Plain of Esdraelon*).[132] Edith Holman Hunt (1847–1930) dedicates the book to their children, Cyril-Benoni and Gladys, who in her narrative are transmuted into three fictitious heroes: Sylvia, Phœbe, and Humphrey Lawson. Her story is based entirely on their actual, day-by-day experiences in Jerusalem, although she also draws liberally upon the latest scholarly authorities and tourist guide-books to describe and interpret various hallowed and historic sites visited by the family.

The house they lived in still stands today in the Street of the Prophets. Her descriptions of furnishing it, local style, vividly recapture the flavor of daily life in Jerusalem in the latter part of the century. For example, the process of transforming the "native" house into "an English home" as seen by her young heroes began in this way:

> First came an old man, whose long white beard would have made him look venerable, were it not for his grotesque white cotton nightcap, with a tassel at the top, which was discovered when his outer cap with its trimming of bushy fur was removed. From underneath this cap there hung on either side of his face a single long ringlet, while all the rest of the head was shaved. On his shoulders he carried a sack, and in his hand a queer instrument of wood and string, something like a bow. He sat himself down in one of the bare rooms, and, emptying a heap of rough cotton from the sack before him, began twanging his bow amongst it, making it in a short time light as a heap of feathers. When the whole sack was finished, he proceeded to tack a bag of linen together with great stitches of string; this was soon made, and filled with the feather-like cotton, then a mattress was complete. This process repeated many times and the house would be furnished with bedding.[133]

The mattress-maker was obviously an orthodox Jew, and the trade he practiced was a common Jerusalem profession which persisted to the days when foam mattresses began to replace the cotton-filled kind. Edith Holman Hunt provides many such vignettes of the local people—mainly tradespeople, "simple folk," and her native servants—with whom she came into daily contact, and incidentally gives us an idea of the schooling of native children in Christian missionary establishments:

> So the house was made ready, but the servants—where were they? Mrs. Lawson [Edith Holman Hunt] looked in vain for girls trained to household work amongst the schools of all creeds which abounded. There were Latins and Greeks, English Protestants and Lutherans.... These [Arab] children could read, write, and sing. They could crochet and sew Berlin wools. They were taken from their poor huts to eat, sleep, and dress like little English children, but never to scrub, sweep, and cook.... It is ever a mistake to assume that one system of training should be applied to all pupils, come they of a barbarous or cultivated race....
>
> The case of the boys in these schools is even worse than that of the girls, for with the adoption of European costume they acquire posts of trust altogether beyond them; they become more skilled in cunning, more bold in their assumed superiority to their more picturesque brethren; those of them who can boast of being "Protestants" seeming to think that the higher rate of wages to which this fact entitles them, is an outward and visible sign of a higher standard of virtue, independent of truth and honesty.
>
> The method of instructing these people should be simple. Just the first principle of truth-speaking ought to be the alpha and omega of training to the children, whose fathers and grandfathers have always looked upon clever lying as proof of extreme superiority.... Mrs. Lawson thought she would set up on a very small scale a home of her own, where...she would make an experiment of training a few Arab girls to real household work, teaching them to clean rooms and windows, wash dishes and saucepans, and the like.... "Do let us have an Arab school, mother," said Sylvia.... "I'm sure we could teach them to speak the truth, and they could teach us to do their lovely needle-work."[134]

How one of the native Arab boys ("these people"), a product of the missionary schools Edith Holman Hunt regards so critically, tells of his life and that of his village childhood friends is presented by Mousa Kaleel, below. At no point did he aspire to a future of

AN ENGLISH HOME IN JERUSALEM.

Hunt, *Children at Jerusalem* (ca. 1880)

serving the needs of Western foreigners that so preoccupied the good lady.

A particularly interesting chapter describes Mrs. Lawson's [the author's] and her children's visit to the harem of a Jerusalem Muslim dignitary:

> …A female Nubian slave stood grinning over the low gate at the entrance to the apartment of the harem…. There was very little ceremony in the introduction of the English guests…. The lady of the harem…and her daughters…led [their vistors] to the upper part of a long low room, round which were set sofas covered with white. A Persian carpet of great beauty covered the centre of the room. There was a low table in one corner, but this was the only furniture. There was no sign of books, work, or music. The room seemed to be arranged for no other use than lounging, and so it truly was.
>
> The mother and daughters…wore their ordinary gay-coloured flannel gowns, with long trains, which they evidently enjoyed to

127

see sweeping the floor as they waddled from side to side, for they were all fat and clumsy.... They threw off all reserve, and questioned Sylvia and Phœbe as to the price of everything they wore, including hair-pins and gloves.... These girls of sixteen were like little children for play, but much less sensible than European little children. They pelted one another with sweetmeats, and were never tired of rolling up cigarettes with great skill. One...was soon to be a bride.... Their enjoyment in all they showed was in telling the price. They never said, "Isn't it lovely?" but always, "It cost such and such a sum."

It was difficult to get away when once within the walls of the harem; and no wonder, for these great ladies are too grand ever to walk, and even when they go out upon donkeys they are so closely

veiled that they can see very little. They clung to their English guests, begging them to stay and sleep there....

"I wouldn't be an Oriental lady for anything in the world," said Phœbe, "not if I could be Mrs. Aladdin even!".... When evening came the children pleaded for an extra half-hour beyond the usual time for going to bed. "Remember we are not Eastern ladies, mother," said Sylvia, "we have such heaps to do!"[135]

Edith Holman Hunt was one of the very few authors of the childrens' books examined here to describe aspects of Arab women's lives. Men were obviously barred from such observations, and few foreign women had opportunities to do so.[136] Due to her actual involvement in local domestic life, Holman Hunt's little book provides lively insights (all too rare in this literature) into the lifestyles of the growing Western community in late 19th-century Jerusalem, and their interrelations with the local people.

Growing up in Jerusalem, 1880s

A delightful, more serious, beautifully written work of this type is Myriam Harry's (1875–1958) *The Little Daughter of Jerusalem*, published originally as a literary magazine serial in French some months before the war in 1914, and later translated into several European languages (an edited Hebrew version appeared in the 1950s). The autobiographical story traces the childhood and early adolescence of "Siona" in the last decades before the turn of the 20th century in Jerusalem. From early childhood Siona [Myriam] was totally captivated by her affectionate, dreamy, handsome father [Moses Shapira, in reality]—a Russian-Jewish convert to the Anglican Church—who was to become notorious as a forger of antiquities. Her German mother was a plain, former Pietist deaconess. Myriam Harry, who subsequently gained recognition as a talented writer in France, at one point relates how she (Siona) became very ill on witnessing a public decapitation by the Ottoman authorities to which she was taken by her earthy native nurse.[137] Her book is full of unusual perspectives from a child's point of view:

> When Siona was nearly five years old, she was carried astride the shoulder of her [Bethlehem Christian] nurse who steadied her by grasping her ankle. Because of the sharp flints on the ground, children, unless riding donkeys, were carried in this peculiar fashion. So, little boys and girls of Jerusalem were accustomed to look down on their surroundings and were never quite like other children.... They were on par with horses' heads, abreast with baskets of anemones and iris, jars of wild honey, and pitchers of curdled milk which the women of Silwan carried on their heads as they strode along. She could almost touch the amulets on the camels' necks. Now and again she caught glimpses of children's faces. Rumias [Eastern Christians] and overdressed little Mussulmans would solemnly look at one another as they passed by, borne shoulder high.[138]

Rather a book about than for children, *The Little Daughter of Jerusalem* contains a wealth of sensitively portrayed local color and

LA PROMENADE DE SIONA, A CALIFOURCHON SUR L'ÉPAULE DE SA NOURRICE

Harry, *La petite fille de Jérusalem* (1914)

Là habitaient les menuisiers qui lui fournissaient les reliures de ses livres en bois d'olivier...

Harry, *La petite fille de Jérusalem* (1914)

vignettes of contemporary life-styles in Jerusalem. The emotions and thoughts of a sharp-witted, mischievous, precocious youngster growing up in the peculiar Levantine Christian-Muslim-Jewish and Arab environment of Jerusalem, make this an indispensable source for the social history of late 19th-century Palestine.

Passages of interest for the local history of Jerusalem, as well as numerous gossipy anecdotal passages telling of her childhood in the eccentric, fundamentalist-Christian American Colony in Jerusalem are also found in Bertha Spafford-Vester's *Our Jerusalem, an American Family in the Holy City, 1881–1949.*[139] Among other reminiscences she tells how, at the age of five, she was dandled by General Charles George ("Chinese") Gordon, "the fabulous hero of the Sudan," who during his prolonged furlough in Jerusalem was a welcome visitor at the American Colony house (now, the

American Colony Hotel). In 1883 Gordon resumed his military duties in the Sudan, and was killed in Khartoum in 1885.

Unlike the hard-working, earthy American youngsters in the Adams colony at Jaffa in the late 1860s, the Holman Hunt children, Myriam Shapira Harry, and Bertha Spafford-Vester were very much upper middle-class, living in households employing many local Arab servants. Although characteristically kind but firm with the native people who catered to their needs and comforts, these authors' outlooks were inevitably elitist in the manner of the general run of the books surveyed in these pages.

Arab children in town and village

Nevertheless, some of the writers who had visited the Scripture lands did note and take interest in the lifestyles of local children. Thus, the open-eyed American, Robert Morris, the author of *Youthful Explorers in Bible Lands* (1870), draws a sympathetic picture of Jerusalem children at play:

> A little girl about six years old, and another little girl about twelve, playing camel, and the big girl is the camel. She kneels down as camels do. Then the little one climbs her back, clasps hands over her forehead, kicks her in the side and makes a noise as cameliers do. The big girl screams and gets up awkwardly, as a camel does, turns her head back, grinds her teeth, spits and shrieks, then away they both go, laughing just as such a merry pair of sisters ought to. All the dress the two girls have on wouldn't cover a candle-stand decently. Their clothes are made of blue cotton of the thinnest, cheapest, and raggedest character. But, oh, what a merry game of camel they do play![140]

Insights into the life and customs of village children in Palestine are provided by John Finnemore in a chapter on "Child Life in the Holy Land" (1908). Among many other observations, always colored by his Western bias, he dwells on the dangerous propensity of Arab boys for throwing stones by hand and with home-made slings, and describes simulation games that undoubtedly reflected the local population's attitudes to tourists passing through the countryside:

> Another favourite game, accompanied by the most tremendous noise, is the representation of an attack upon peaceful travellers by a band of Bedouin robbers. This is a very popular game, and the travellers, a band of boys, leading one or two donkeys they have fetched from the village pastures, are assailed by a yelling horde of their comrades, who swoop upon them from cover, after the style of Arab robbers, and a mimic battle is joined.[141]

An insider view from Ramallah, 1890s-1908

A very different, most important and revealing work in this respect is *When I Was a Boy in Palestine* (1914), in the "Children of Other Lands" series published by Lothrop, Lee & Shepard of Boston. Mousa Kaleel (1892–19..), a young Christian Arab from Ramallah, graphically describes his village childhood and schooling in missionary establishments of the Society of Friends (which function there to this day).

SYRIAN BLINDMAN'S BUFF.
The players call it "Jacob and Rachel."

Kaleel, *When I was a Boy in Palestine* (1914)

133

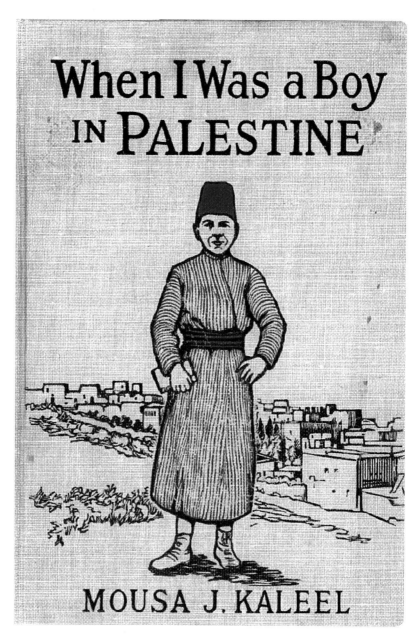

Book cover: Kaleel, *When I was a Boy in Palestine* (1914)

At the mission school, the ambitious youngster was taught "the dignity of labor, and respect for useful knowledge and its exercise in any worthy form." The school fostered student self-government along American democratic principles, the students forming a voluntary organization that they named (in Arabic) the "Against-Things-Harmful Society" to develop character and good conduct. At the age of sixteen Mousa Kaleel left his home to join his elder brother who had emigrated to the United States. He attended a preparatory school in Maine, and worked his way through Haverford College in Pennsylvania. He was a diligent student and star football player. One thing, however, that troubled young Mousa in his studies in America was working under women teachers. Eventually, due to failing eyesight he went into business—with apparent success.

In his small but solidly-packed book, Mousa Kaleel devotes several incisive chapters to his own family and to the activities of children at play, work, and elementary schooling in rural Ramallah. He portrays in detail the agricultural year and its festivities, Arab village customs, discusses proverbs and other folklore, the various religious and ethnic groupings, and the Turkish government of Palestine as it affected the ordinary Arab inhabitants. Although not uncritical of his own people, he writes with gentle humor and great understanding and pride in his cultural heritage. Thus, at one point, Kaleel judiciously but firmly reproves one traveler through Palestine who called Arab peasants "the worst people in the East," and who cited "as an added proof of the depravity of the people, an incident of being abused in 'the most scurrilous language' by the children!":

> Boys in Palestine, I must admit, are fighters, and are taught by their parents to fight. This is justified by the internal conditions of the country, caused by a very weak and slack government. The boy must grow into a man who has a good aim with his gun, and who can hurl a stone a great distance with accuracy. It is a semi-primitive land, and men have to live accordingly to get along in it. The people are good at heart and often blessed with the keenest brains in the world; all they need is some gentle leadership…willing…to

135

lift them up gradually. It is natural that they should resent any "Khawaja" (upper-class foreigner) trying to make a curiosity of them, continually shooting at them with clicking cameras, and asking insolent and prying questions about their sanctuaries. Many of the tourists who visit Palestine do so from a desire to study the religious customs of the people...and they thoughtlessly offend the people by making light of what are very sacred things. The lowliest peasant in Palestine is vain, and the tiniest boy can throw a stone. With these as acknowledged facts let the missionary and investigator work.[142]

Elsewhere, Kaleel writes about biblical Palestine, as he saw it:

Palestine is a veritable land of memories. It was the principal theatre of Biblical history.... For this reason the study of Palestine is a recognized aid to the better understanding of the Bible.

Every saint may claim a shrine in Palestine, and then many will be left over for the non-saints. Such is the amazing number of holy places that tourists weary of looking at them and hearing stories about them.... And although indicated by tradition only, which in most cases cannot be precisely verified, and may even be rendered doubtful by scientific inquiry, these places still have a charm for us, for what spot in the little land could have escaped being hallowed by some incident, recorded or forgotten? Thus the country, the people, even the very atmosphere, remind us of Biblical things.[143]

In terms of the realities of the Holy Land, Mousa Kaleel's unpretentious, straightforward little book is a rare ray of light among the general murkiness of idealized, woolly preconceptions, and often considerable ignorance of the countries and people in the general run of this literature. The work stands out also among the few books written by those Westerners well-acquainted with the country whom we have met in this chapter. Kaleel's book provides inside knowledge of the lives of the native inhabitants as told by one of them who acquired a Western education. Despite a certain depth of understanding evinced by Edith Holman Hunt, Myriam Harry, and Bertha Spafford-Vester, they remained essentially outsiders, securely bound to their Western cultural and class roots and preconceptions. Mousa Kaleel's book is therefore not typical of the juvenile literature on the Holy Land. But then, it

Mousa J. Kaleel (1892–19..)

fully bears out its Boston publishers' advertising claim for their "Children of Other Lands" series of which it was part:

There are many books *about* the children of other countries, but no other group like this, with each volume written by one who has *lived* the foreign child life described, and learned from subsequent experience in this country how to tell it in a way attractive to American children—and in fact to Americans of any age.

137

Eddy, *Walter in Jerusalem* (1863)

138

IV.

IDEALS AND CONVENTIONS

WHAT then are the educational objectives permeating the general body of this English and American juvenile literature on the Holy Land throughout the century-and-a-half under review, be it religious or recreational, travelogue or fictionalized historical writing, or even based on personal experiences? With due allowance for the characteristic, contemporary conventions and styles of the different sub-periods, the social attitudes running through most of these works represent a fairly consistent thread.

In addition to stressing the "manliness" or "lady-like accomplishments," fortitude, self-reliance, craving for useful knowledge, and Christian piety of their young heroes, many of these books glorify evangelical missionary endeavors as selfless Christianizing and civilizing labors. A number of the writers were clergymen, lay leaders, or even missionaries themselves. Samuel and Amy Zwemer, who served in Bahrein and Oman, dedicate their book, *Zigzag Journeys in the Camel Country* (1911), "To the children of missionaries all the world over," and invite their young readers to "make many a new zigzag track across the map of Arabia to mark your journeys as future missionaries."[144] All of these books published until the 1860s, and later ones as well, aspire at forming what was perceived to be the ideal Christian character. In the earlier books, as has been seen above, even plots mainly emphasizing adventure are replete with examples and illustrations of filial duty and obedient respect for elders, religious faith, love of the Scriptures, as well as the inevitable pursuit of "useful knowledge." In *The Little Pilgrims in the Holy Land* (1861), one of the last of those books to reflect puritan preoccupations with good Godliness, the precariousness of human life on earth, and salvation of the soul, the Reverend Henry S. Osborn of Philadelphia rather morbidly concludes his narrative of Amy, Ettie, Rose, Sallie, Mary, Willie, and Fannie's trip through the Holy Land with the words: "…I hope to see you, my dear little friends, when, as holy pilgrims to the Happy Land, you have finished your course, and have triumphed, and safely arrived at your home in heaven."[145]

The social outlook of the overwhelming majority of these works is decidedly elitist. It reflects the fact that those able to afford overseas travel and the luxurious camping facilities in Egypt and the Holy Land provided by Thomas Cook and other tourist agencies, came from the social, political, and business aristocracy of the industrial nations. Already two decades before the onset of organized tourism, Barbara Hofland had, in the 1820s, characterized her young hero's father, the elder Mr. Campbell, as a "gentleman from a beautiful part of Perthshire, affluent in his fortune, beloved by his tenantry…."[146] Other children in these stories are sons and daughters of well-to-do Boston and New York merchants, of a noted Orientalist and professor of archeology, of an exporter who made his fortune in Brazilian coffee, of a famed missionary doctor and scholar, of a ranking British officer in the Indian army, and the like. Mary Wade's *Twin Travellers in the Holy Land*, "…wide-awake American boy and girl of twelve years, make the most of their wealthy uncle and aunt's invitation to accompany them on a trip through the Holy Land."[147] And Miss Spark, a young woman of humbler origins from Machiasport, Maine, who has "not the faintest conception that there is an impropriety in going about the world unprotected," is willy-nilly accepted as a traveling companion by the Hales' *Family Flight* Horner and Stuyvesant families, even though she is "not exactly well-bred, in the society sense of the word" and wears a preposterous "green travelling dress, buttoned behind."[148]

Implicit in the many passing references to the degradation of the "natives," to the inferiority of "colored peoples," the filth in public places, and the misgovernment, apathy, and venality of the Turkish rulers is the concept that was to be immortalized by Rudyard Kipling in 1899 as the "White Man's Burden." Responsibility for the enlightenment (with a benevolent but resolute hand) of backward races is held up as an important ideal for American children as it is for those of Britain and the European powers. "If Christians owned the Holy Land, it would be clean;" "Yankee enterprise and British capital would soon cover the Sea of Galilee with steamboats and yachts;" "Seeds for change will only be sown by foreign residents;" "England is expert in managing the affairs of eastern nations;" and many other such declaratory statements permeate this literature.[149] A few of the authors, however, did temper their harsh assessments with compassion:

> "You should rejoice, boys," remarked Mr. Percy, "that God has given you your birth in America instead of in this country; you, perhaps, would be what these poor creatures are if you lived here. Their condition should excite your pity and commiseration, and not your contempt...That they are so filthy is an evidence that they are degraded, and their degradation is pitiable. You should have your hearts filled with gratitude to your kind Father in Heaven for giving you a higher and better idea of life, and placing you in a land full of privileges and blessings."[150]

A rare, more balanced view in these children's books of the relative merits of Western and Oriental moral principles is expressed by Thomas W. Knox, a much-traveled writer of vast personal experience with "primitive" peoples (and with little illusions about his own kind):

> One of the boys asked the Doctor if this was a part of the race of Arabs that made it unsafe for travellers to go through their country. "Yes," answered the Doctor. "I do not know that this particular camp indulges in robbery, but the chances are that it does. The Bedouin of Syria and Palestine have their own notions about the

141

rules of life, and with most of them robbery is not incompatible with honesty."

The boys [Frank Bassett and Fred Bronson] laughed at this idea, and then the Doctor explained his meaning. "You are aware," said he, "that among the Indians of our Western plains it is perfectly legitimate to steal horses; we might come nearer home and say that many respectable men in New York and other cities do not think they have done anything wrong when they persuade their friends to buy the stocks and other property that they wish to sell. The rules of honesty vary in different parts of the world, and the standard of one country or people will not always answer for another."[151]

From the time of the British occupation of Egypt in 1882 and the wars in the Sudan, English children's books become even more empire-oriented and patriotic (but not necessarily jingoist) than they had been in the wake of Napoleon's defeat.[152] Political bias regarding the other great powers expressed in American children's books set in the Levant is more ambiguous. Napoleon Bonaparte's campaigns in Egypt and Palestine are invariably rendered as evil and cruel, albeit with some admiration for his military genius and due regard for the archeological discoveries.[153] On one occasion, France's discomfiture by Britain in attempts to expand her presence in the region is a source of amusement to the young travelers.[154] But England is seen as pursuing a "dog in the manger" policy in Egypt by not allowing a foothold to the other powers, and keeping Egypt in abject—if efficiently administered—submission.[155] Before the outbreak of World War I, when all the American and—of course—the English children's books completely identify with the Allied cause, the mention of Germany evoked no particular opinions, and certainly no negative ones. There is however no ambivalence in any of the Christian juvenile books as to the pernicious nature of Turkish government, and the desirability of speeding its inevitable demise.

Prejudices and conceptualizations

> Lord, I ascribe it to Thy Grace,
> And not to chance, as others do,
> That I was born of Christian race,
> And not a heathen or a Jew.
>
> (Isaac Watts, "Song VI," *Divine and Moral Songs for Children, 1715*)

By far the most offensive characterizations in this purportedly "wholesome" educational writing are reserved for the people of Palestine and the adjacent lands. Muslims, Jews, and Christians of all but Protestant denominations are generally depicted in uncomplimentary terms. Even assessments aspiring to fairness tend to be patronizing. There could be no doubt in the minds of young readers of these books as to their own innate superiority over the people described.

Muslim Arabs and Bedouin

With the notable exception of Mousa Kaleel's first-hand, personal descriptions of the life of Arab village children without any religious differentiation, Arab Muslims, as distinct from Christian Arabs, are portrayed by most of the authors in extremely negative terms as fanatical, uncouth, dirty, greedy, cheating, and untruthful: "The Arabs are a lazy race of people; even Yusuf, the donkey boy, who tries hard to do right, likes better to sit and suck sugar-cane than to work."[156] Or, in a lighter vein: "This is a yelling people. They say *yellah* to a horse to make him move, and they are always yelling when they talk."[157] And,

> The Arabs say that when the Father of Lies came on earth to distribute his goods he had nine bagfuls. He spread one bag of lies in Europe, and then started for Asia and Africa. He landed in Egypt one evening, intending to scatter one bagful over that country and Syria, and then go on the next day to Asia; but while he slept the Arabs stole all his remaining stock, and distributed it among themselves. This accounts for the great difficulty they have in telling the truth.[158]

143

The hatred of Christians ("giaours") by the local population, especially in the hill country of Samaria, subjects several of the young heroes of these children's books to volleys of stones thrown by Arab boys, calling forth manly recourse to "eight-inch Colts" to "produce good effects...[by] impressing the Arabs with the perfection of American and English weapons."[159] Each bullet is good for an Arab,[160] there is some eagerness for "a little brush with natives,"[161] and for being "as ready to shoot a Bedouin as a squirrel."[162] Good words for Arabs usually take the form of praising those who prove faithful servants and efficient dragomans.

In this literature, the Bedouin of the desert regions fare somewhat better on the whole than the Muslim Arabs of town and village. Some authors indeed eschew a romanticizing view:

> A great deal of nonsense has been written about the noble character of the Bedouin Arabs, their bravery, scrupulous honor, and other commendable qualities. Of course there are exceptions, and it would be strange indeed if a people numbering many thousands should all be rascals. But, taken as a whole, the Bedouin are a race of thieves, and their few redeeming traits are not sufficient to offset their bad qualities.[163]

Yusuf and "Mark Twain"
Hunt, *Yusuf in Egypt* (1878)

But few of the writers could resist the lure of the Bedouin sheikh in flowing white robes galloping to battle on his pure-bred Arab steed. He never failed to stir the imagination, and increasingly found his way into the more adventure-oriented books for young-sters—as in other Western literature. Thus, Edgar Blagrove, Hen-ty's intrepid young hero of *At Aboukir and Acre*, saves the life and becomes the blood brother of Sidi, the son of Sheikh Ben Ouafy. Consequently, he is taken in for a time by the tribe, learning Bed-ouin ways and joining the tribesmen in fighting the French inva-ders of Egypt.[164] Although uncomplimentary generalizations about Bedouin abound ("He glories especially in taking by stealth...what he is not strong enough to seize by force...they are very cunning rogues..."),[165] they do have redeeming virtues: "Bad as...[they] are, they never rob or injure a guest.... With them a guest is sacred.... A sheikh will drive as hard a bargain for guiding you as he can, but once a bargain is made he will be faithful."[166] The author of *Boy Travelers in Arabia*, the Reverend Dr. D. Wise who was a Methodist missionary, made it a didactic point to include the following passage:

> "...There is one Arab virtue which even a Boston boy may properly emulate."
> "What is that, sir?" inquired both lads, speaking simulta-neously.
> "Temperance," replied their tutor, "Arabs do not touch strong drink."[167]

The Bedouin come fully into their own in Lowell Thomas's account for boys in his journalese version of T.E. Lawrence's exploits in World War I. As they did earlier in Henty's tale of the fighting against Napoleon Bonaparte's troops in Egypt, the Bedouin serve as willing instruments in the British cause.[168] With great gusto they ambush, kill, and plunder Turks at Lawrence's instigation (and liberal distribution of gold sovereigns and Enfield rifles) as part of the strategic and tactical planning of the Arab Bureau in the Cairo headquarters of the British army.

The religion of Islam is rarely dealt with, and then rather

cursorily ("It is a cheerless creed, if creed it can be called....").[169] Only from the end of the 19th century on do some of these children's books express a more sympathetic attitude toward the local Muslim population.[170] It was a direct result of persistent evangelizing missionary educational efforts among Eastern Christian Arabs in Syria and Palestine and of growing apprehension at the effects of dynamic ("materialistic") Zionist settlement activity on their particular conception of the "Holy Land."[171] Thus, in 1897, the missionary, William L. Worcester, in his story of Jesus' childhood, gives his boyhood comrades Arabic names—Ali, Ahmed, Khalil, etc.—with the obvious intent of disavowing any positive Jewish connection.[172]

Nevertheless, the Princeton Theological Seminary and the Theological Seminary of Reformed Churches in America and its American Mission in Cairo were deeply concerned with the conversion of Muslims. A leading advocate of missionary work among Muslims was Samuel Marinus Zwemer (1867–1952). The titles of some of his polemical, ideological works speak for themselves: *Mohammed or Christ; an Account of the Rapid Spread of Islam in all Parts of the Globe, the Methods Employed to Obtain Proselytes, its Immense Press, its Strongholds, & Suggested Means to be Adopted to Counteract the Evil* (ca. 1915), *The Cross Above the Crescent; the Validity, Necessity and Urgency of Missions to Moslems* (1941), and others of like import. As mentioned above under "Books for younger children," among Zwemer's publications are also small "educational" volumes for children he wrote together with his wife, Amy: *Topsy Turvy Land; Arabia Pictured for Children* (1902), and *Zigzag Journeys in the Camel Country. Arabia in Picture and Story* (1911).[173]

Jews

While there is no lack of pejorative characterizations ("...the Jews I know by their noses;"[174] on Jews in Tiberias: "generally a worthless and lazy lot;"[175] "...a hard-faced Jew, whom the boys dubbed Shylock;"[176] etc.), on the whole, a condescending, ambivalent atti-

Eddy, *Walter in Jerusalem* (1863)

tude to Jews runs through all of this literature. Visits to the Western ("Wailing") Wall in Jerusalem were a "must" on every tourist itinerary. On the one hand, the young American hero of Daniel Eddy's "Walter's Tour in the East" series is moved by the sight of devout Jews at the Wall:

> "What chapter are they reading?" asked Walter.
> "The ninth of Jeremiah," replied his father. Walter drew out his English Bible, and finding the place, read with them aloud. Then

147

the Jews went up to the wall and kissed it, and the boys saw that the rough wall had been kissed smooth by Jewish lips.

"Shall I go and kiss the wall, pa?" asked Walter.

"If you please, my son."

"Oh, don't be so foolish, Walter," said Harry.

"I want to do as they do. I sympathize with them, and pity them."

"What for?"

"Because they are shut out of the Temple which their fathers loved so much."...Walter went forward and kissed the stones, and the Jews looked at him in surprise....[177]

But in summing up the discussion of his heroes' encounter with the Jews of Jerusalem, and the broader implications regarding Jews in general, the author readily reverts to common stereotypes:

"What do you think of the Jews?" asked Harry.

"A peculiar people," answered Dr. Forestall. "Their whole history is peculiar. Their sojourn in Egypt, their flight into the wilderness, their conquest of this land, their wars with the Philistines, their captivity in Babylon, their rejection of the Messiah, and their subsequent dispersion—all make them a very interesting people."

"They have been much persecuted, have they not?"

"Yes, they have.... The Jew has always been feared, hated, and detested. When we hear of a Jew, we are apt to suppose he is an extortioner, or wicked man."

"Are there not some good Jews?"

"O yes; many. Some of the most noted men of the world belong to that outcast race. The Rothschild family—those rich bankers that you have heard so much about—are Jews.... We often give the Jews a worse character than they deserve...."

"They were once a great and illustrious people" [said Walter]. "Why do not all the Jews throughout the world come here and buy up this land, and redeem it from the rule of the Arabs, and set up a new Jewish government?.... Do not many persons believe that the Jews will at some time return?.... I have become much interested in this outcast race, of which we see so much, and which is suffering so much...."[178]

And similarly: "Of course," exclaimed Mamma, "they [the Jews] will come back to their own land, body as well as soul.... How I

148

should like to live and see them all back here!" "Yes," said Charlie; "and no one can deny that they have more money than any other nation of earth."[179]

The Jewish Question is the main theme of *Three Vassar Girls in the Holy Land*, published in Boston in 1892, as one of a series of travelogue stories in different countries by Mrs. Elizabeth W. Champney. "Lizzie" Champney introduces lengthy passages from standard tourist guide-books and travel accounts to pad the treacly plot written for genteel teen-age girls. In this case, the heroine, Bird Orchard, is an accomplished student at Vassar who has been hiding her Jewishness and real name of Zipporah Baumgarten in order to conform to the social atmosphere at the school. She is invited to join two of her school companions in the party of one of their well-to-do families in a trip through Egypt, Sinai, and Palestine. Her secret is gradually revealed in the course of their travels through chance encounters with her overtly Jewish parents in Jerusalem, where her father is employed in acquiring land for Jewish settlement.[180] The story well illustrates the common anti-semitic prejudices and stereotypes current in American society, with the author taking pains to show these up as unfair and un-justified:

> "Mother!" Frank exclaimed in a tone of real anguish, "...What possible disgrace is there in the fact that Bird is a Hebrew? I consider it, on the contrary, an honor that she can trace her ancestry back for ages to a race that gave us Christ and the Christian religion, and which alone held the true knowledge of God, and was noted for its refinement and learning when our own ancestors were besotted savages."
>
> Mrs. Remington shrank visibly before this outburst. "Yes, I know," she muttered feebly; "you love her Frank,...and I don't wonder, for she is very bewitching; and if this is not generally known, I don't think it need make any difference...but I fear society would hardly look at her Hebrew connections in that way."[181]

What however really redeems Bird-Zipporah in the eyes of her American friends is that she eventually shows signs of recognizing Jesus as the true Messiah.

Far more characteristic of the way the Jews of Palestine are portrayed in these books is the description by Barton Johnson in 1892: "...We met many Jews in the streets, and were struck by their peculiar dress.... They were a sallow, unhealthy looking race, and were said to be very dishonest and tricky. Indeed, we could not expect to find a very noble people living in so foul a place [as Tiberias]."[182]

The youthful travelers (in body or spirit) through the Holy Land are invariably conducted on visits to missionary establishments dedicated to the conversion of Jews:

> ...Then there is the hospital of the Jewish Mission, where they have twenty-five beds or more for the sick Jews, and give them every comfort, but do not try to convert them while they are sick. The poor people feel it, and it leaves a soft corner in their hearts for Christians.[183]

And:

> "...I have always thought the Jews would be converted through the instrumentality of the English and American races," said papa. "...We must visit Solomon's Pools again and see the Garden of Urtas!.... The ground is cultivated by a converted Jew, and he has proved what Jews can do if they are trained to agricultural pursuits."[184]

As in the case of Bird (Zipporah Baumgarten) Orchard, the crypto-Jewish heroine of the *Three Vassar Girls in the Holy Land*, conversion of Jews and Muslims to Protestant Christianity—in laudable recognition of the true faith—seems an almost compulsory theme to be incorporated in much of this literature. Thus, Yusuf, the little orphaned Egyptian (who had named his beloved donkey, "Mark Twain") is taken to America by his wealthy tourist benefactors to be trained for the ministry.[185] Even in the essentially non-religious, historical adventure books published in the late 19th and early 20th century, the theme of conversion to Christianity is introduced—if rather perfunctorily—by Henty who is remarkably free of anti-Jewish bias, and more extensively, with decided anti-semitic innuendos, by Haggard, into their action-filled narratives

150

based on Josephus. So, for example, in *For the Temple*, after the defeat of his people, Henty's young Jewish hero of the revolt against Rome joins the new sect of followers of the martyred teacher from Galilee.[186]

The ambivalent attitudes to Jews conveyed to young readers in these works sometimes result in incoherent statements deriving from a confused understanding of Jewish history, as in the following description in 1909:

> ...Nor do the Jews who live in Palestine to-day descend from the Hebrews who fought for the Temple, and were butchered in thousands by the Roman soldiery. The Jew of to-day is for the most part an immigrant. He has returned to the land of his fathers from exile, and often forms part of some colony fostered by the wealth of some Jewish millionaire....[187]

(The logic here is puzzling: If the modern Jews are not descended from the "Hebrews" of the Second Temple period, how and why would they "return from exile" to "the land of their fathers"?)

"Other" Christians

At the hands of the Protestant writers for children considered here, Catholics are at best depicted with disdain: "...I suppose [said Sallie]...they do some good by entertaining travellers in the convents." "I don't know what good these do; but I know some Roman Catholic priests in past years have been very good men, although I don't quite see how they could be."[188] And, "Of course we treated their [the Roman Catholic monks in Nazareth] stories with due respect, and refused to laugh in their faces...."[189]

Eastern Christians hardly fare better: Copts are labeled "cheats and nominal Christians,"[190] and Greek monks and Armenians are portrayed as wily and treacherous[191]—in one case trying to convert a steadfast young English lad to their faith which entails belief in saints, images, and other "superstitions."[192] A Greek monk named Basil is characterized as "about the biggest blackguard in Jerusalem," who, among his other misdeeds, "stabbed a Franciscan last year at Easter time—you know they're always scrapping, these Holy Sepulcher monks. And he runs a fake relic factory in Bethlehem—turns out crosses and rosaries by the ton...." He was "one of the most powerful and one of the wickedest men in Jerusalem. His eyes were cruel, his manner was insolent."[193]

Many of the books mention the thousands of poor Russian-Orthodox pilgrims footslogging their way from holy site to holy site throughout the length and breadth of the country in the sweltering springtime heat, kissing every cross and prostrating themselves in front of every icon:

RUSSIAN PILGRIMS IN THE HOLY LAND.

Knox, *The Boy Travellers, Egypt and the Holy Land* (1882)

> Pilgrims from all parts of the Christian world are in Jerusalem; most of these are Russians in long boots and heavy fur clothing. Greek priests with their chimney-pot hats are seen all over the city, selling candles and souvenirs and extorting coins..., and by the time the pilgrims are ready to depart for the land of the Great Bear, these contemptible priests have stripped them of all their money and even the choice pieces of fur that make parts of their clothing.... When the robbery is complete, the Russian Consul is called upon to pay for the return passage of several thousand benighted pilgrims.[194]

"You see, Willie dear," explains the ever-moralizing Auntie Hetty, "these poor creatures [the Russian and Greek pilgrims and rapacious monks] are altogether misguided.... Their religion does not change the heart...as pure religion does. It does not say to them, as ours does 'And be ye kind to one-another'...."[195]

The wickedest man in Jerusalem.

Moffett, *The Land of Mystery* (1913)

"Turkey is inhabited by a very singular people,
called Turks. Their dress, houses, food, and
customs are all singular. They wear turbans instead
of hats, and loose robes instead of coats...."

Goodrich, *Peter Parley's Tales About Asia* (1830)

The *"Unspeakable Turk"*

Ever since the Turkish tribes of Central Asia that adopted Islam appeared on the Middle Eastern scene in the early Middle Ages—and especially after the Ottoman conquests in Europe and the Mediterranean lands in the 16th and 17th centuries—fear and abuse, and consequent dehumanization of the "Turk" had become endemic in European folk and cultural tradition. From the late Middle Ages on, there has been a confusion of the terms "Turk," "Saracen," "Arab," and "Mohammedan," to the point where "to turn Turk" meant becoming a Muslim.[196] Accordingly, one writer, in his tale of the Third Crusade for children published in 1885, has no qualms about having his twelve-year-old hero, Eric, appeal to King Richard's Christian sensibilities: "Sir King!...let me go with you to the Holy Land! I will get a little sword and cut off the heads of all the Turk boys, and then they will never grow up into Turk Soldiers."[197]

In almost all the juvenile literature reviewed here, by far the

TURKISH ARMY DISCIPLINE.

(Leyell), *A Run Around the World* (1891)

most vehement disparagement is reserved for the Turkish rulers. Thus, in one case, when young travelers come across remains of well-built, ancient Roman roads and inquire of their mentor as to the cause of their destruction, he attributes it (rather simplistically and at least in part erroneously) to

> The neglect of twelve hundred years. When this country was conquered by the Arab Mohammedans, they saw no need of wagon roads.... Nor have the Turks ever been road builders. It is their policy to get as much out of a country as possible, and leave as little as possible. Nor have the crushed and hopeless inhabitants had the spirit to build roads of their own will.[198]

The following, written in the early 1880s, is typical:

> "I hate those Turks!" exclaimed Richard...
> "Yes, they are a blood-thirsty race," said the professor, smiling at the vehemence of his two pupils. "And yet, I hardly think we ought to *hate* them; though they have been a scourge to the lands

155

they rule. Still it is our part not to hate, but to pity them for their wickedness and for the woes they thereby bring upon themselves; but their *punishment* belongs to the God of nations, who in due time will smite them with his avenging sword."

"And his terrible sword," the doctor remarked, with a solemnity which made the boys start, "is already out of its scabbard. The doom of the pitiless Turk hangs over him like a storm-cloud ready to burst."

"...the Turks, though once brave and powerful, have almost run their race. Their best qualities have departed; their vices only flourish, and it will not be long before they will cease to be rulers, either in Europe or Asia."[199]

And this general tenor is invariably maintained right into World War I:

...The Turk is the worst governor in the world. He has only one idea, and that is to fill his own pockets. A Turkish governor may see very clearly that by...laying heavy taxes on a poor country he is bringing it to utter ruin, that in a short time there will be no more taxes for anybody to gather, but for all that he seizes everything he can lay hands on at the moment, careless of the future. But even worse than the weight of the taxes is the method of their collection....[200]

One of the few authors who tries to draw a more balanced picture of the Turks encountered by his "Youthful Explorers in the Holy Land" is Robert Morris, who as in other matters, prefers to rely on his own first-hand experiences rather than on common stereotypes. He notes the natural courtesy of ordinary Turkish soldiers, and makes friends with the Turkish governor of Jaffa—who happens to be a fellow Freemason—"a good man" whose "manners are unexceptionable."[201]

Respect for nature and historical assets

Not surprisingly, considering the prevailing smugness characteristic of the period regarding man's power over the elements, nature as well as historic and holy sites are considered expendable. At a visit to the traditional house of Simon the Tanner "by the seaside" in Jaffa (Acts 10:6), Harry cries, "Out with your hammer, Walter!" causing the latter to hack away gleefully at one of the ancient walls until "he had secured several good specimens, which he divided round among the party," and "No one prevented them (the young pilgrims) from breaking off pretty specimens of the [beautiful Corinthian] marble carving" at Tyre.[202]

As to wildlife, birds and animals, edible or not, are shot for sport and to show off marksmanship. Thus, "Every traveller up the Nile thinks it his bounden duty to…shoot a crocodile, but not one in a hundred is successful."[203] In one case, to the disappointment of Mr. Lawson (William Holman Hunt), hunting down a magnificent eagle soaring over the Mount of Olives at sunset [fortunately] failed, as did an attempt to capture a hyena alive.[204]

Education to an awareness of natural values and assets, and of responsibility for preserving unique historical man-made environments was still far off in the future: the very concept of nature and historical conservation only took on momentum after the mid-20th century.

DUCK-SHOOTING ON THE NILE.

Butterworth, *Zigzag Journeys in the Levant* (1886)

V.

SUMMARY

Except for those very few works written from protracted, first-hand experience in the Holy Land, the juvenile books surveyed above have little or no importance as original historical or geographical source material. But there can be no question of their value as significant social documents for their time, for children's books "have always been particularly vulnerable to the ideologies of the age"[205] and, in this case, faithfully reflect the spirit, the conventional attitudes, and the educational philosophy of the self-righteous American and British elites that produced them. This writing represents a distillation of the tenets and values which parents, teachers, and religious mentors saw fit to inculcate in young minds regarding the particular subjects considered here.

Because of the religious connotations of the Holy Land, the temper of these books changed with contemporary trends and fashions at a slower pace than in the evolution of other popular writing for children. Nevertheless, earlier emphasis on pious and didactic subject matter was increasingly enlivened by adventure motifs derived from the published experiences of explorers and travelers in Bible lands. The eventual displacement of Protestant Christian religious content by secular and imperial-national themes, and later, the circumscribed introduction of more respectful attitudes to differing peoples, was in line with the general social and cultural developments in England and America in the latter decades of the 19th century, through World War I, and its aftermath. Although American juvenile books on the Holy Land probably outnumber the ones by British authors, there was a constant, lively interchange between the two kindred nations. Nor is it at all certain that more of the English books were also published in America than American books in England. Despite some differences in outlook and style there would be little point in treating them separately.

One contemporary American educator, presumably representing a consensus of pedagogic opinion, considered books of this kind to be "most agreeably written and incredibly wholesome."[206] And in England, a reviewer for the *Christian Leader* of a Henty action volume thought that: "Morally, the book is everything that could be desired, setting before the boys a bright and bracing ideal of the English gentleman."[207] Until the last decades of the 19th century most of the authors, about one-third of them women, probably unconsciously and as a matter of course, directed their writing at children and youngsters of the wealthier classes. Only when the masses were drawn into the excitement of imperialist wars and national honor did working-class heroes and characters begin to appear in these books. Although it is hard to establish from existing evidence, even in small doses this literature undoubtedly helped shape the attitudes of persons from elitist Anglo-Saxon social environments, and later also from the lower social classes, toward Muslims, Arabs, Turks, other Christian denominations, and—not in the least—to Jews and their restoration to their ancient homeland and to the Zionist movement. The overall approach to the people of Palestine, that must have been almost universally held in Britain, the United States, and in the major European countries, is epitomized concisely in the following passage by Edith Holman Hunt in her *Children at Jerusalem*:

> ...The Arabs through whom Europe received her traditions of ancient learning were a race possessing a kingly intellect, but under the dominion of the Turk, any race, however fine, would become enslaved, and consequently degraded. Their brains have dimin-

ished, since the use of them has been directed simply to eluding oppression, and fostering cunning as the chiefest virtue....The good folks [the Christian missionaries] who are already at work act upon the fiction that Arabs, Jews, and English are the same but for training, while all experience proves that, teach them as you will, the old inherent nature is only modified, not destroyed. A Jew, for instance, although a convert, may be a better Jew, but he is still a Jew; and an Arab is still an Arab.[208]

Or, in more general terms, as Robert Louis Stevenson put it so engagingly and succinctly in the concluding verse of his children's poem "Foreign Children":

> Little Turk or Japanee,
> Oh! don't you wish that you were me?

Thus, in these children's books the realities of the Middle East fade before stereotyped preconceptions and mental images that ultimately stemmed from the authors' own religious and cultural conditioning regarding the "East."[209] It is hardly to be expected that any of this writing would attempt to see things through the eyes and minds of the "natives" in the countries described. The occasional redeeming passages expressing a measure of sympathy, compassion, and understanding have more of condescension about them than broad-mindedness. And, all considered, how many children are likely to make allowances for viewpoints other than those implanted in their consciousness?

Assessing the actual impact of this literature is problematic. Henty wrote in the *Boys' Own Paper* in 1902 that army officers and volunteers for active service assured him that his books were instrumental in encouraging enlistments—"not so much into the rank and file as among the officers."[210] If the estimated figure of 25 million copies of Henty's books sold is indeed correct, and considering that they were accessible in school and public libraries to a much wider readership, those volumes dealing with the Middle East constituting three to five percent of his output must have been read in the hundreds of thousands.

161

Conceivably, among youngsters growing up with these and others of the books surveyed here as part of their reading were some who later in life came to influence, determine, conduct, and serve British and American policies in the Middle East at various levels—from statesmen and politicians to soldiers and minor officials. Through them, to a lesser or greater degree, the juvenile literature dealing with that part of the world may also have affected the destinies of the people in the region.

HOME AGAIN.

Eddy, *Walter's Tour in the East* (1865)

NOTES

1. Although some works in French and German are considered here, this survey essentially focusses on English and American books. The books and articles mentioned in the text are listed chronologically in Part A of the Bibliography. The alphabetical listing, Part C of the Bibliography, includes also titles and editions not discussed in the text. The titles listed in Part A are preceded by an asterisk * in Part C. See also Part B of the Bibliography—"General Background Works Consulted." References to books of incidental relevance to the text are given only in the notes.

2. Rosenbach, *Early American Children's Books*, pp. xxvi-xxvii.

3. For good overviews of English and American children's literature see: Arbuthnot & Sutherland, *Children and Books*; Avey, *Children and Their Books*; Darton, *Children's Books in England*; Kiefer, *American Children Through Their Books*; Meigs, *A Critical History of Children's Literature*; Muir, *English Children's Books*; Thwaite, *From Primer to Pleasure*; etc.

4. Avey, "The Puritans and their Heirs," p. 95; Muir, *English Children's Books*, pp. 226–227, remarks that "until the eighteen-fifties and even later a carefree attitude unencumbered by moral or instructional preoccupations was strikingly exceptional in writing for children."

5. Darton, *Children's Books in England*, pp. 215*ff.*

6. Various editions of given titles are indicated in Part C. of the Bibliography at the end of this survey.

7. The following background sketch draws on standard works, among them: E.C. Black (ed.) *Victorian Culture and Society*, New York, 1973; R.A. Divine (ed.), *American Foreign Policy*, Cleveland, 1970; R.C.K. Ensor, *England 1870–1914*, Oxford, 1963; E. Halévy, *A History of the English People in the Nineteenth Century*, London, 1961; G. Himmelfarb, *Victorian Minds*, New York, 1968; E.R. May, *Imperial Democracy. The Emergence of America as a Great Power*, New York, 1961; S.E. Morison, *The Oxford History of the American People*, New York, 1965; M. Plesur, *America's Outward Thrust. Approaches to Foreign Affairs 1865–1890*, De Kalb, 1971; etc.

8. The writer James Russell Lowell who served as the American minister to the Court of St. James, quoted in Plesur, *America's Outward Thrust*, p. 52 (see Note 7, above).

9. May, *Imperial Democracy*, p. 27 (see Note 7, above).

10. The Congregationalist minister Josiah Strong quoted in ibid., p. 8. Edouard Demolins's *Anglo-Saxon Superiority: To What It Is Due* was an attempt by a Frenchman to assess the nature of this special relationship.

11. Quoted in May, *Imperial Democracy*, p. 53 (see Note 7, above).

12. W.R. Wilson, *Travels in the Holy Land, etc.*, 3rd ed. London, 1831, p. 198 (and see Note 34, below).

13. Mme. Savary, *Letters on Egypt*, Dublin, 1787; Lady Mary Wortley Montagu, *Letters*, London, 1720; Baron F. de Tott, *Mémoires*, Maestricht, 1785.

14. Adams, *Flowers of Modern Travels*.

15. Draper, *Bible Illustrations*, pp. iv-v.

16. Quoted in: Darton, *Children's Books in England*, p. 216.

17. R. Pococke, *Description of the East and some Other Countries*, London, 1743-5; E.D. Clarke, *Travels in Various Countries of Europe, Asia and Africa*, Cambridge, 1810-23.

18. Hack, *Oriental Fragments*, pp. v-vi.

19. Draper, *Bible Illustrations*, pp. 4-5, 182-183.

20. Kiefer, *American Children*, pp. 61-62.

21. Gregg, *Selumiel*, pp. 109-110.

22. Alexander, *Uncle Austin and His Nephews*, p. 177.

23. Goodrich, *Peter Parley's Tales About Asia*, p. 99.

24. Haviland, *The Travelogue Storybook*, pp. 6-8; Darton, *Children's Books in England*, pp. 227ff.

25. Darton, *Children's Books in England*, pp. 224; Kiefer, *American Children Through their Books*, pp. 24-25; Meigs et al, *A Critical History of Children's Literature*, pp. 141-145; etc.

26. Hofland, *The Young Pilgrim*, pp. iii-v.

27. Hofland, *Alfred Campbell*, pp. 6-8.

28. Darton, *Children's Books in England*, pp. 215-216; and see: T. Ramsay, *Life and Literary Remains of Barbara Hofland* and *Memoir of the Life and Literary Remains of Mrs. Hofland*.

29. Hofland, *Alfred Campbell*, p. iii.

30. See Note 34, below.

31. Hofland, *Alfred Campbell*, pp. iii-iv.

32. Hofland, *The Young Pilgrim*, p. vii.

33. U.J. Seetzen, *Reisen durch Syrien, Palästina, etc.*, Berlin, 1854-9 (English translations of several of Seetzen's reports appeared in 1813); J.L. Burckhardt, *Travels in Syria and the Holy Land*, London, 1822; J.S. Buckingham, *Travels in Palestine, etc.*, London, 1822. Good summary works on Palestine explorers and travelers are: F.J. Bliss, *The Development of Palestine Exploration, being the Ely Lectures for 1903.*

London, 1906; Y. Ben-Arieh, *The Rediscovery of the Holy Land in the Nineteenth Century*, Jerusalem, 1979.

34. C.L. Irby & J. Mangles, *Travels Through Nubia, Palestine and Syria in 1817 and 1818*, London, 1823 (and several other editions); E.D. Clarke, *Travels in Various Countries of Europe, Asia, and Africa*, Cambridge, 1810–23 (and several other editions, including an American one in 1814) (see also Note 17, above); F.A. de Chateaubriand, *Itinéraire de Paris a Jérusalem, etc., etc.*, Paris, 1811 (and many subsequent editions, including an American one in 1814); W.R. Wilson, *Travels in the Holy Land, Egypt, etc.* London, 1822 (and other editions); F. Henniker, *Notes During a Visit to Egypt, Nubia, the Oasis, Mount Sinai and Jerusalem*, London, 1823.

35. Hofland, *The Young Pilgrim*, pp. 79*ff*; F. Henniker, *Notes During a Visit to Egypt, Nubia, the Oasis, Mount Sinai, and Jerusalem*, London, 1823, pp. 285–287.

36. Hofland, *The Young Pilgrim*, pp. 89–90.

37. Ibid., pp. 116–117, 132.

38. For example, compare the passages quoted above with Irby and Mangles, *Travels, etc.* (see Note 34, above), pp. 244, 384, etc., etc. Long after Mrs. Hofland's death, in the 1880s, passages and ideas from her Alfred Campbell books were plagiarized and "recycled" in turn, almost word-for-word, by the Rev. P.W. Raidabaugh in his Holy Land travel book for youngsters, *The Pilgrims; or, Uncle Joseph and Rollin Through the Orient*, published by the Evangelical Association in Cleveland (e.g., pp. 10–11).

39. Stille, *Alfred Campbell*.

40. Peploe, *The Travels and Adventures of Charles Durand*, pp. 2, 4.

41. Ibid., pp. 178–179.

42. Hofland, *The Young Pilgrim*, pp. 210–211.

43. Darton, *Children's Books in England*, p. 254.

44. Röhricht, *Bibliotheca Geographica Palæstinæ*, relying partly on Tobler, lists 40–50 titles of school texts on biblical geography for the period 1792–1877, mostly in German, but also in French, English, Dutch, etc. See also Note 45, below.

45. The standard bibliography of Palestine literature: Röhricht, *Bibliotheca Geographica Palæstinæ*, lists nearly two thousand titles for the period 1800–1877. It is, however, far from being complete, nor does this number include all the different editions of any given work. The total quantity of such material for the 19th century is probably closer to twice that number, and the output from the year 1878 on continued at an even greater pace.

46. Rae, *The Business of Travel*, pp. 171–172.

47. Mark Twain (Samuel L. Clemens), *The Innocents Abroad*, Hartford, 1869, pp. 482–484. Mark Twain refers to and pokes fun here at an earlier book, *Tent Life*

in the Holy Land, New York, 1857, by William C. Prime (thinly disguised by Mark Twain as "Wm. C. Grimes").

48. Robert Morris, *Freemasonry in the Holy Land*, La Grange, Ky., 1879, pp. 476–477.

49. See for example: Kark, *American Consuls in the Holy Land*, pp. 247–250.

50. Tilt, *The Boat and the Caravan*, p. 287.

51. Among the authors of juvenile books on the Holy Land and Egypt discussed in this survey, who also published books for the general public on their travels, were: H.S. Osborn (*Palestine Past and Present*, Philadelphia, 1859, and others); R. Morris (*Freemasonry in the Holy Land*, New York, 1872); T.W. Knox (*The Oriental World. A Record of Travel and Observation*, Hartford, 1878, and others); D.C. Eddy (*Eddy's Travels in Asia and Africa*, Boston, 1893); H.R. Haggard (*A Winter Pilgrimage, Being an Account of Travels Through Palestine, Italy, and the Island of Cyprus, Accomplished in the Year 1900*, London, 1904); A. Goodrich-Freer (*Inner Jerusalem*, London, 1904; and *Arabs in Tent and Town*, London, 1924); C. Moffett (*The Land of Mystery. A Story of Palestine Describing a Ride from Jerusalem to Damascus*, New York, 1920); and L.J. Thomas (*With Lawrence in Arabia*, Garden City, N.Y., 1924).

52. Eddy, *Walter in Athens*, pp. 220–226; Butterworth, *Zigzag Journeys in the Levant*, pp. 68–75, 268–271; Johnson, *Young Folks in Bible Lands*, p. 90.

53. Morris, *Youthful Explorers*, pp. 30–31.

54. Eddy, *Walter in Athens*, Note; *Walter in Egypt*, Preface.

55. Eddy, *Walter in Jerusalem*, pp. 99–100.

56. Butterworth, *Zigzag Journeys in the Levant*, Preface.

57. Quoted in the publisher's prospectus for the series, Hale & Hale, *A Family Flight*, end pages.

58. Johnson, *Young Folks in Bible Lands*, p. 3.

59. For example: O.R. Seward (ed.), *William H. Seward's Travels Around the World*, New York, 1873; J.R. Young, *Around the World with General Grant....*, 2 vols., New York, 1879; F.E. Clark, *Our Journey Around the World. An Illustrated Record of a Year's Travel*, Hartford, 1895; R. Meredith, *Around the World on Sixty Dollars*, Chicago, 1901; and many others.

60. See Note 51, above.

61. Quoted in Haviland, *The Travelogue Storybook*, p. 19.

62. Quoted in ibid., p. 20.

63. Ibid., pp. 33–40.

64. See also: ibid., p. 24.

65. See Notes 48 and 51, above.

66. See below, under "American youngsters in Jaffa." Morris visited the group shortly before its final dispersal.

67. Morris, *Youthful Explorers*, p. 5.

68. Ibid., p. 64.

69. Ibid., p. 30; and see Kark, *American Consuls in the Holy Land*, pp. 290–291 on the import of petroleum products to Palestine from the U.S.

70. Morris, *Youthful Explorers*, pp. 134–135.

71. Ibid., p. 202.

72. *National Union Catalog*, 396:108, Entry 0794433.

73. (John Leech Porter), *Handbook for Travellers in Syria and Palestine*, London: Murray, 1858, pp. xiii-lxvi.

74. See Note 51, above.

75. Osborn, *The Little Pilgrims*, pp. 232–233.

76. Ibid, p. v.

77. Eddy, *Walter in Samaria*, p. 51.

78. Mark Twain, *The Innocents Abroad*, p. 511.

79. Haviland, *The Travelogue Storybook*, p. 57.

80. See Note 51, above.

81. Quoted in the end-pages of Wade, *Our Little Turkish Cousin*.

82. Finnemore, *The Holy Land*, pp. 4–5.

83. Douglas, *The Land Where Jesus Christ Lived*, p. 219.

84. Zwemer, *Topsy Turvy Land*, pp. 29, 46, 67.

85. Quoted in: Haviland, *The Travelogue Storybook*, p. 58.

86. Carpenter, *Our Little Friends of the Arabian Desert*, p. 18.

87. Douglas, *The Land Where Jesus Christ Lived*, pp. 38–41.

88. Martineau, *Times of the Saviour* New Edition, 1870, pp. vi-vii. Other books for children on the Life of Jesus and the Apostles have not been included here since they are not really relevant to this survey.

89. Adapted from *Théatre à l'usage des jeunes personnes*, par madame la comtesse de Genlis. (St. John, *The Osborne Collection*, 2:758.) Mme. de Genlis, who wrote tirelessly on many subjects, including on "moral education," seems to have had a special predilection for the desert. Another of her dramatized developments of biblical passages—of rather sensuous character (for adults)—centered on Moses' relations with Jethro's daughters (*Les bergères de Madian, ou la jeunesse de Moïse.*

Nouvelle édition. Paris: Maradon, 1821). For local color on Sinai the author drew on some of the 18th century travel literature, such as Carsten Niebuhr's *Voyage en Arabie*, the French version of which was published in 1776–80.

90. Johnstone, *The Wars of the Jews*, p. vi.

91. Peploe (Mrs. J.B. Webb), *Naomi*, p. 5.

92. Ch. Mills, *The History of the Crusades, for the Recovery and Possession of the Holy Land* 2 vols., London, 1820; Richard of Devizes, Geoffrey de Vinsauf, Lord John de Joinville, *Chronicles of the Crusades, Being Contemporary Narratives of the Crusade of Richard Cœur de Lion, and of the Crusade of Saint Louis*, London: Bohn, 1848; T.A. Archer & C.L. Kingsford, *The Crusades. The Story of the Latin Kingdom of Jerusalem*, London, 1894; John of Wuerzburg, *Description of the Holy Land (A.D. 1160-70)*, P.P.T.S., London, 1896; Beha ed-Din, *The Life of Saladin (1137-1193 A.D.) or, What Befell Sultan Yusuf*, P.P.T.S., London, 1897; S. Lane-Poole, *Saladin and the Fall of the Kingdom of Jerusalem*, London, 1898; and others.

93. Th. Fuller, *Historie of the Holy Warre*, London, 1639 (reprinted in 1840); and see: H. von Sybel, *The History and Literature of the Crusades*, transl. from German and edited by Lady Duff Gordon, London, 1841 (1865?)

94. Hanson, *A Travel Book for Juniors*, p. 61. And see, for example: Vivian Gilbert, *The Romance of the Last Crusade with Allenby to Jerusalem*, London & New York, 1923.

95. Scott, *The Talisman*, p. vi.

96. J. Carne, *Letters from the East*, London, 1826. This information appears in the Preface to the Philadelphia: McKay (n.d.) edition of *The Talisman*, p. v, and in other editions.

97. Scott, *The Talisman*, pp. 1–2.

98. Guiding Star, "Bathing in the Dead Sea," *The Children's Friend* VIII (1873) 11: 341–342.

99. Scott, *The Talisman*, p. 33; and see also: Said, *Orientalism*, pp. 60, 101–102, 169.

100. See discussions of such literature in: Huttenback, *The British Imperial Experience*, pp. 92–95; Gross & Springhall, "The Mystique of Empire," pp. 295–301; Katz, *Rider Haggard and the Fiction of Empire*. A good summary of Henty's life and work is provided in Carpenter & Prichard, *The Oxford Companion of Children's Literature*, pp. 244–247.

101. Fenn, *George Alfred Henty*, pp. 321, 334.

102. See Note 51, above.

103. Henty, *At Aboukir and Acre*, pp. 195–196, 211.

104. Henty, *The Young Midshipman*, pp. 185–187.

105. Moffett visited Palestine and wrote about his travels; see Note 51, above.

106. Moffett, *The Land of Mystery*, p. 394.

107. Ibid., p. 213.

108. C.L. Woolley & T.E. Lawrence, *The Wilderness of Zin*, London: P.E.F. Annual, 1915; E. Huntington, *Palestine and its Transformation*, Boston, 1911.

109. For example: W.T. Massey, *The Desert Campaigns*, London, 1918; and idem., *How Jerusalem was Won, being the Record of Allenby's Campaign in Palestine*, London, 1919; *A Brief Record of the Advance of the Egyptian Expeditionary Force under the Command of General Sir Edmund H.H. Allenby, G.C.B., G.C.M.G. July 1917 to October 1918*, London: H.M. Stationery Office, 1919.

110. Brereton, *With Allenby in Palestine*, pp. 81, 87, etc.

111. Ibid., p. 79.

112. Thomas, *The Boys' Life of Colonel Lawrence*, p. 9.

113. Wade, *Twin Travellers*, p. 15.

114. Wade, *Our Little Jewish Cousin*, from the Preface of the pre-World War I editions, pp. v-vi.

115. Ibid. "Introduction" added to the eleventh impression, October 1925, pp. iii-iv.

116. Hanson, *A Travel Book for Juniors*, p. 66.

117. Ibid, p. 168.

118. Charlton, *Near East Adventure*, p. 10.

119. Bell, *The Sacred Scimiter*, pp. 120-121, 247-248.

120. (Ch. Kingsley), *Letters and Memories*, London 1879, New York, 1900, Vol. I, pp. 374-375.

121. Quoted in Carpenter & Prichard, *Oxford Companion to Children's Literature*, p. 246.

122. W.E. Houghton, *The Victorian Frame of Mind*, New Haven, 1959.

123. Hunt, *Children at Jerusalem*, pp. 7-8.

124. This phenomenon is subjected to meticulous scrutiny in Said, *Orientalism*, and subsequent analyses; and see also the introductory chapter "America and the Holy Land—Concepts" in: Kark, *American Consuls in the Holy Land*.

125. Douglas, *The Land Where Jesus Christ Lived*, p. 190. And see also Alexander, *Uncle Austin and his Nephews*; and to a lesser extent also in Eddy's "Walter's Tour in the East" series, and some of the other travelogue and fictional historical adventure books discussed here.

126. Hofland, *The Young Pilgrim*, pp. 73-74; Hale & Hale, *A Family Flight*, p. 277.

127. Tilt, *The Boat and the Caravan*, pp. v-viii, 8-9.

128. Ibid., pp. 111–114.

129. For a comprehensive treatment of this episode see: R.M. Holmes, *The Forerunners*. Independence, Mo., 1981.

130. Quoted in: Chamberlain, "A New England Crusade," pp. 197, 202–203. I am grateful to Jean Carter of Pepperell, Mass. for a copy of this article.

131. From the manuscript *Chronicles of Edwin R. McKenzie*, Jaffa, Syria. I am grateful to Jean Carter for permission to reproduce some of this unpublished material.

132. Edith Holman Hunt, née Waugh, was a distant relative of the writer Evelyn Waugh. See, among others: W. Holman Hunt, *Pre-Raphaelitism and the Pre-Raphaelite Brotherhood*, London, 1902; Diana Holman-Hunt, *My Grandfather, His Wives and Loves*, New York, 1969.

133. Hunt, *Children at Jerusalem*, pp. 46–47.

134. Ibid., pp. 49–55.

135. Ibid., pp. 59–69.

136. For an incisive feminist view of Bible lands travel literature, see: Melman, *Women's Orients*. I am grateful to Ruth Roded for bringing this to my attention.

137. Harry, *La petite fille de Jérusalem*, pp. 12–16.

138. Ibid., p. 8 [my free translation from the French, J.S.].

139. First published by Doubleday in Garden City, N.J., 1950; and see pp. 96–98 for the following passages on General Gordon.

140. Morris, *Youthful Explorers*, p. 158.

141. Finnemore, *The Holy Land*, pp. 16–17, 60–66.

142. Kaleel, *When I Was a Boy in Palestine*, pp. 22–24.

143. Ibid., pp. 136–137.

144. Zwemer, *Zigzag Journeys in the Camel Country*, p. 17.

145. Osborn, *The Little Pilgrims*, p. 298.

146. Hofland, *Alfred Campbell*, p. 1.

147. Wade, *Twin Travellers*, front endpaper.

148. Hale & Hale, *A Family Flight*, pp. 270–275.

149. See for example: Eddy, *Walter in Samaria*, p. 208; *Walter in Constantinople*, pp. 12–28; *Van Wert's Travels*, p. 114; Knox, *The Boy Travellers*, pp. 48–49; Willard, *Along Mediterranean Shores*, pp. 87–88; Wade, *Twin Travelers*, p. 13; etc.

150. Eddy, *Walter in Samaria*, p. 50.

151. Knox, *The Boy Travellers*, p. 329.

152. See for example: (Anonymous), *The English in Egypt*; Henty: *At Aboukir and Acre*, *The Young Midshipman*, *The Dash for Khartoum*, *With Kitchener in the Soudan*, etc.

153. For example: Eddy, *Walter in Jerusalem*, p. 20; Morris, *Youthful Explorers*, pp. 9, 31, 56; etc.

154. Knox, *The Boy Travellers*, p. 15.

155. Hale & Hale, *A Family Flight*, pp. 70–71; Butterworth, *Zigzag Journeys in the Levant*, p. 210. In the case of the Hales, this attitude may probably be attributed to the views held by their brother Charles, who at the time served as the United States consul at Alexandria. In this context, a passing remark in Morris, *Youthful Explorers*, p. 115, (written in 1870, more than a decade before the British occupation of Egypt) is interesting: "I am glad to learn from [twelve year-old] Elliot that the childish prejudice against the English, which he has expressed, sometimes offensively, is now removed. Most of our American boys imbibe this feeling to some extent from their school-books of history."

156. Hunt, *Yusuf in Egypt*, p. 209.

157. Morris, *Youthful Explorers*, p. 31.

158. Knox, *The Boy Travellers*, p. 273.

159. Eddy, *Walter in Samaria*, p. 65.

160. Eddy, *Walter in Egypt*, p. 22.

161. Eddy, *Walter in Samaria*, p. 49.

162. Eddy, *Van Wert's Travels*, p. 171.

163. Knox, *The Boy Travellers*, p. 333.

164. Henty, *At Aboukir and Acre*, p. 17; and see above, under: "Henty and the imperialists."

165. Wise, *Boy Travelers in Arabia*, p. 57.

166. Ibid., pp. 59–60.

167. Ibid., p. 100.

168. Thomas, *The Boys' Life of Colonel Lawrence*; and see above, under: "The First World War and the Palestine Mandate."

169. Wise, *Boy Travelers in Arabia*, p. 175. Passages describing Islam, the life of Muhammad, and early Muslim history appear in Eddy, *Walter in Damascus*, pp. 167–188; Adams (Oliver Optic), *Asiatic Breezes*, pp. 290–309; Carpenter, *Our Little Friends of the Arabian Desert*, pp. 183–184, 190–192, 198–201; and in very few other such works.

170. Kaleel, *When I Was a Boy in Palestine*; Zwemer, *Topsy-Turvy Land, Childhood in the Moslem World*, and *Two Young Arabs*; Thomas, *The Boys' Life of Colonel Lawrence*.

171. Handy, *The Holy Land in American Protestant Life*; Kark, *American Consuls in the Holy Land*.

172. W.L. Worcester. *Children of Gospel Days*. Philadelphia: American New Church Tract and Publication Society, 1897. This interesting observation was noted by Vogel, "Zion as Place and Past." I am grateful to Ruth Kark for drawing my attention to this passage.

173. See: Bibliography, Parts A and C, under ZWEMER.

174. See Note 113, above.

175. Knox, *The Boy Travellers*, p. 389.

176. Johnson, *Young Folks in Bible Lands*, p. 355.

177. Eddy, *Walter in Jerusalem*, pp. 84-85.

178. Ibid., pp. 190-197.

179. Knight, *Ned Harwood's Visit to Jerusalem*, p. 119.

180. Champney, *Three Vassar Girls*, pp. 188-189.

181. Ibid., p. 254.

182. Johnson, *Young Folks in Bible Lands*, p. 171.

183. Knight, *Ned Harwood's Visit to Jerusalem*, p. 144.

184. Ibid., p. 145.

185. Hunt, *Yusuf in Egypt*, pp. 217-218. The author was a Southern Methodist active in the Temperance Society.

186. Henty, *For the Temple*, pp. 368-370; and see above, under: "Henty and the imperialists."

187. Finnemore, *The Holy Land*, pp. 2-3.

188. Osborn, *The Little Pilgrims*, p. 245.

189. Johnson, *Young Folks in Bible Lands*, p. 144.

190. Eddy, *Walter in Egypt*, p. 210.

191. Moffett, *Land of Mystery*, pp. 113, 115, 129, 181, etc.

192. Peploe, *The Travels and Adventures of Charles Durand*, p. 81

193. Moffett, *The Land of Mystery*, p. 128-129.

194. Kaleel, *When I Was a Boy in Palestine*, pp. 132-133.

195. Douglas, *The Land Where Jesus Christ Lived*, p. 215.

196. See, for example: P. Coles, *The Ottoman Impact on Europe*, London, 1968, pp. 145*ff.*

197. Harrison, *Brothers in Arms*, p. 10.

198. Johnson, *Young Folks in Bible Lands*, p. 94.

199. Wise, *Boy Travelers in Arabia*, pp. 40, 72.

200. Finnemore, *The Holy Land*, p. 5.

201. Morris, *Youthful Explorers*, pp. 11–21.

202. Eddy, *Walter in Jerusalem*, p. 21; Osborn, *The Little Pilgrims*, p. 163.

203. For example: Morris, *Youthful Explorers*, pp. 82–83, 101–102; Hale & Hale, *A Family Flight*, p. 133; Tilt, *The Boat and the Caravan*, p. 80; etc.

204. Hunt, *Children at Jerusalem*, pp. 76–81.

205. Avey, "The Puritans and their Heirs," p. 95.

206. Robert Morss Lovett, "A Boy's Reading Fifty Years Ago," *The New Republic* 48 (1926) 623:334, quoted in Haviland, *The Travelogue Storybook*, p. 25.

207. Quoted in Carpenter & Prichard, *Oxford Companion to Children's Literature*, p. 246.

208. Hunt, *Children at Jerusalem*, p. 54.

209. See Note 124, above.

210. Quoted in Carpenter & Prichard, *Oxford Companion to Children's Literature*, p. 246.

BIBLIOGRAPHY

Note:

The Bibliography is in three parts: Part A.—a short, chronological list of books on the subject under discussion that are mentioned in the text; Part B.—general background works consulted; and Part C.—an expanded bibliography of Christian juvenile works on the Holy Land and adjacent regions published until the mid-1930s, mainly in English but also in other languages, listed alphabetically by author. Ancillary works referred to in the notes but only indirectly relevant to this survey are not repeated in the Bibliography. The foregoing discussion and generalizations have been based entirely upon this material, which, however, makes no claim to being complete. Additional works, especially books in other languages, and from Catholic and other non-Protestant viewpoints, may modify some of the present conclusions.

*

A. Chronological, short listing of works mentioned in the survey

GENLIS, Stéphanie Félicité de. *Hagar in the Desert*. Translated from the French for the use of Children. Worcester, Mass.: Isaiah Thomas, 1785.

ADAMS, John (Reverend). *The Flowers of Modern Travels; being Elegant, Entertaining and Instructive Extracts, Selected from the Works of the Most Celebrated Travellers, etc. Intended chiefly for Young People of both Sexes*. Boston: John West, 1797.

JAMIESON, Mrs. (late Miss Frances Thurtle). *Popular Voyages and Travels, throughout the Continent and Islands of Asia, Africa, and America*. London: Whittaker, 1820.

HOFFLAND, Barbara. *Theodore, or the Crusaders. A Tale for Youth*. London: Harris, 1821.

JOHNSTONE, Mrs. Christina Jane ("Aunt Jane"). *The Wars of the Jews as Related by Josephus, Adapted to the Capacities of Young Persons*. London: Harris, 1823.

SCOTT, Walter. *Tales of the Crusades*. Edinburgh: Constable, 1825.

HOFLAND, Barbara (Wreaks Hoole). *Alfred Campbell; Containing Travels in Egypt and the Holy Land*. London: Harris, 1825.

HOFLAND, Barbara. *The Young Pilgrim, or Alfred Campbell's Return to the East and his Travels in Egypt, Nubia, Asia Minor, Arabia Petræa, &c &c...* London: Harris, 1826.

HACK, Maria. *Oriental Fragments*. London: Harvey & Darton, 1828.

STILLE, Caroline (ed.). *Alfred Campbell, oder Reisen eines jungen Pilgers nach Aegypten und dem gelobten Lande.* Hamburg: Campe, 1830.

GOODRICH, Samuel Griswold. *Peter Parley's Tales About Asia.* Boston: Gray & Bowen, Carter & Hendee, 1830.

DRAPER, Rev. Bourne Hall. *Bible Illustrations; or, A Description of Manners and Customs Peculiar to the East, Especially Explanatory of the Holy Scriptures.* London: Harris, 1831.

(GREGG, Jarvis). *Selumiel, or, A Visit to Jerusalem.* Philadelphia: American Sunday School Union, 1833.

ROBINSON, Edward. *A Dictionary of the Holy Bible, for the Use of Schools and Young Persons.* Boston: Crocker & Brewster, 1833.

ALEXANDER, James Waddell. *Uncle Austin and His Nephews or, The Scripture Guide.* Philadelphia: American Sunday School Union, 1838.

PEPLOE, Annie (Molyneux; Mrs. J.B. Webb). *Naomi; or, The Last Days of Jerusalem.* London: Ward, Locke & Bowden, 1840.

HOFLAND, Barbara. *Alfred Campbell; or Travels of a Young Pilgrim in Egypt and the Holy Land.* New edition with additions. London: Newman, 1841.

PEPLOE, Annie (Molyneux; Mrs. J.B. Webb). *The Travels and Adventures of Charles Durand.* London: Danton, 1847.

(TILT, Charles). *The Boat and the Caravan; a Family Tour Through Egypt and Syria.* London: Bogue, 1847.

HAWKS, Francis L.. *Richard the Lion Hearted.* New York: Dickerson, 1855.

ABBOTT, Jacob. *History of King Richard the First of England.* New York: Harper, 1857.

PEPLOE, Annie (Mrs. J.B. Webb). *Naomi; or, The Last Days of Jerusalem* New Edition (17th ed.). London: Routledge, 1860.

OSBORN, Henry S. *The Little Pilgrims in the Holy Land.* Philadelphia: Challen, 1861.

ANDREWS, Jane. "Gemila and Alee, the Child of the Desert" in: *The Seven Little Sisters Who Live on the Round Ball That Floats in the Air.* Boston: Ticknor & Fields, 1861.

EDDY, Daniel Clarke. *Walter's Tour in the East. Walter in Egypt; Walter in Jerusalem; Walter in Samaria; Walter in Damascus; Walter in Constantinople; Walter in Athens.* New York: Sheldon, 1863–1865.

YONGE, Charlotte Mary. *The Prince and the Page; a Story of the Last Crusade.* London & Cambridge: Macmillan, 1866.

McKENZIE, Edwin R. *Chronicles of Edwin R. McKenzie.* Indian River, Maine: unpublished manuscript, 1867.

BOWMAN, Anne. *The Young Nile Voyagers*. London: Routledge, (1868).

ALEXANDER, Barbara (Mrs. Hutton). *Heroes of the Crusades*. London: Giffith & Farran, (1868).

MORRIS Robert. *Youthful Explorers in Bible Lands*. Chicago: Hazlitt & Reed, 1870.

MARTINEAU, Harriet. *Traditions of Palestine: Times of the Saviour* New Edition. London: Routledge, 1870.

HUNT, Sara Keables. *Yusuf in Egypt; and His Friends*. New York: American Tract Society, 1878.

ANDREWS, Jane. "What Was Gemila Doing All This Time" in: *Each and All; or, How the Seven Little Sisters Prove Their Sisterhood*. Boston: Lee & Shepard: 1878.

HOFLAND, Barbara. *Theodore; or the Crusades*. London: Griffith & Farran, 1879.

HUNT, Mrs. (Marion Edith) Holman. *Children at Jerusalem: A Sketch of Modern Life in Syria*. London: Ward, Lock, (1881).

HALE, Edward Everett & Susan Hale. *A Family Flight over Egypt and Syria*. Boston: Lothrop, 1882.

EDDY, Daniel Clarke. *Rip Van Winkle's Travels in Asia and Africa by Rupert Van Wert*. New York: Crowell, 1882.

CHAPLIN, Fannie P. and HUMPHREY, Mrs. Frances A. "Zumetta" (a little Arab girl) pp. 7–18; "Muggerditch's Trowsers" (a little Turkish boy) pp. 31–38; "Little Folks in Egypt" pp. 50–58, in: *Little Folks of Other Lands*. Boston: Lothrop, Lee & Shepard, 1882.

HENTY, George Alfred. *Winning His Spurs; A Tale of the Crusades*. London: Low, Marston, Searle & Rivington, 1882.

KNOX, Thomas Wallace. *The Boy Travellers. Adventures of Two Youths in a Journey to Egypt and the Holy Land*. New York: Harper, 1883.

WISE, Daniel. *Boy Travelers in Arabia: or, From Boston to Bagdad*. New York: Phillips & Hunt, 1885.

HARRISON, F. Bayford. *Brothers in Arms. A Story of the Crusades*. London: Blackie, 1885.

BUTTERWORTH, Hezekiah. *Zigzag Journeys in the Levant, with a Talmudist Story-Teller. A Spring Trip of the Zigzag Club Through Egypt and the Holy Land*. Boston: Estes & Lauriat, 1886.

(ANONYMOUS). *The English in Egypt with a Full and Descriptive Life of General Gordon, the Hero of Khartoum and Other Pioneers of Freedom*. London: Sangster, (1886).

CHAMPNEY, Elizabeth Williams. "10th Transformation—to an Egyptian Child" and "20th Transformation—to a Syrian Girl—Damascus," in: *The Bubbling Teapot, A Wonder Story* by "Mrs. Lizzie W. Champney." Boston: Lothrop, n.d. (1886).

HENTY, George Alfred. *For the Temple; a Tale of the Fall of Jerusalem.* London: Blackie, 1887.

RAIDABAUGH, P.W. *The Pilgrims; or, Uncle Joseph and Rollin Through the Orient.* Cleveland: Evangelical Association, 1887.

KNIGHT, Susan G. *Ned Harwood's Visit to Jerusalem.* Boston: Lothrop, 1888.

EVERARD, William. *Sir Walter's Ward. A Tale of the Crusades.* London: Blackie, 1888.

ALEXANDER, Barbara (Mrs. Hutton). *Tales of the Saracens.* London: Giffith & Farran, 1890.

DOUGLAS, Hester. *The Land Where Jesus Christ Lived.* London: Nelson, 1890.

HENTY, George Alfred. *The Young Midshipman. A Story of the Bombardment of Alexandria.* London: Blackie and New York: Scribners, 1890.

(LEYELL, Henry). *A Run Round the World or The Adventures of Three Young Americans.* Boston: De Wolfe, Fiske & Co., 1891.

CHAMPNEY, Elizabeth Williams. *Three Vassar Girls in the Holy Land.* Boston: Estes & Lauriat, 1892.

JOHNSON, Barton Warren. *Young Folks in Bible Lands.* St. Louis: Christian Publishing Co., 1892.

HENTY, George Alfred. *At Aboukir and Acre; a Story of Napoleon's Invasion of Egypt.* New York: Scribners, 1898.

GLEE, Prof. *A Journey Round the World, Including Interesting Adventures in Many Lands with Professor Glee and His Class of Young People in Their Travels.* (Place not given): W.E. Scull, 1901.

STRATTON, Ella (Hines). *Our Jolly Trip Around the World with Captain Parker, or The Lucky Thirteen and Their Long Voyage of Discovery in Search of Knowledge.* Philadelphia: National Publishing Co., (1902).

ZWEMER, Samuel Marinus & Amy Elizabeth (Wilkes). *Topsy Turvy Land; Arabia Pictured for Children.* New York: Revell, 1902.

HOLLIS, Gertrude. *A Slave of the Saracen. A Tale of the Seventh Crusade.* London, Edinburgh, New York: Nelson, n.d. (ca. 1902).

HAGGARD, Henry Rider. *Pearl-Maiden, a Tale of the Fall of Jerusalem.* New York: Collier, 1902.

CHANCE, Lulu Maude. "Ahmed, the Arabian Boy" pp. 66–81, in: *Little Folks of Many Lands.* Boston, New York, Chicago, London: Ginn, 1904.

HAGGARD, Henry Rider. *The Brethren. A Romance of the Time between the Second and Third Crusades*. London: Cassel, 1904.

WADE, Mary Hazelton (Blanchard). *Our Little Jewish Cousin*. Little Cousin Series; Boston: Page, 1904.

WADE, Mary Hazelton (Blanchard). *Our Little Turkish Cousin*. Little Cousin Series. Boston: Page, 1904.

CHAMBERLAIN, George Walter. "A New England Crusade" in: *New England Magazine* 36 (1907) 2: 195–207.

MANSFIELD, Blanche (Mc Manus). *Our Little Arabian Cousin*. Boston: Page, 1907.

MANSFIELD, Blanche (Mc Manus). *Our Little Egyptian Cousin*. Boston: Page, 1908.

FINNEMORE, John. *Peeps at Many Lands—The Holy Land*. London: Black, 1908.

HOLLIS, Gertrude. *Between Two Crusades. A Tale of A.D. 1187*. London: Society for the Promotion of Christian Knowledge, (1908).

SWEETSER, Kate Dickinson. "Stephen and Nicholas: Boy Crusaders." In: *Ten Boys from History*. New York & London: Harper, 1910.

ZWEMER, Samuel M. & Amy E. *Zigzag Journeys in the Camel Country. Arabia in Picture and Story*. New York: Revell, 1911.

GOODRICH-FREER, Adela M. (Mrs. Hans Henry Spoer). *Things Seen in Palestine*. London: Seely, Service, 1913.

MOFFETT, Cleveland. *The Land of Mystery*. New York: Century, 1913.

HARRY, Myriam (Mme. Emile Perrault-Harry). *La petite fille de Jérusalem*. Paris: Arthème Fayard, 1914.

KALEEL, Mousa J. *When I was a Boy in Palestine*. Boston: Lothrop, Lee & Shepard, 1914.

WILLARD, Mary Frances. *Along Mediterranean Shores*. Boston: Silver, Burdett, 1914.

ZWEMER, Samuel Marinus. *Childhood in the Moslem World*. New York: Revell, 1915.

ROLT-WHEELER, Francis. *The Wonder of War in the Holy Land*. Boston: Lothrop, Lee & Shepard, 1919.

WADE, Mrs. Mary Hazelton (Blanchard). *Twin Travelers in the Holy Land*. New York: Stokes, 1919.

BRERETON, Frederick Sadleir. *With Allenby in Palestine*. London & Glasgow: Blackie, (1920).

HANSON, Helen Patten. *A Travel Book for Juniors*. New York, Cincinnati, Chicago: Abingdon, 1921.

WADE, Mary Hazelton (Blanchard). *Our Little Jewish Cousin* 11th impression, October 1925, with new Introduction.) Boston: Page, 1925.

ZWEMER, Amy Elizabeth (Wilkes). *Two Young Arabs; the Travels of Noorah and Jameel.* West Medford, Mass.: The Central Committee on the Study of Foreign Missions, 1926.

GOODRICH-FREER, Adela M. (Mrs. Hans Henry Spoer). *Things Seen in Palestine.* New and Revised Edition, London: Seely, Service, 1927.

STABLES, William Gordon. *For Cross or Crescent. The Days of Richard the Lion-Hearted. A Romance.* Glasgow & Birmingham: Hulbert, 1927.

THOMAS, Lowell Jackson. *The Boys' Life of Colonel Lawrence.* New York & London: Century, 1927.

KING, Marian. *Amnon: A Lad of Palestine.* New York: Behrman, 1931.

CARPENTER, Frances. *Our Little Friends of the Arabian Desert, Adi and Hamda.* New York, Boston, etc.: American Book Co., 1934.

CHARLTON, Lionel Evelyn Oswald (Air Commodore). *Near East Adventure.* London: Nelson, (1934).

BELL, William Dixon. *The Sacred Scimiter.* Chicago: Goldsmith, 1938.

LEVINGER, Elma Ehrlich. *Pilgrims to Palestine and Other Stories.* Philadelphia: Jewish Publication Society of America, 1940.

B. General background works consulted

ARBUTHNOT, May Hill and SUTHERLAND, Zena. *Children and Books.* 4th ed. Glenview, Ill.: Scott, Foresman, 1972.

ATKINSON, Caroline P. (ed.). *Letters of Susan Hale* (Introduction by Edward E. Hale). Boston: Marshall Jones, 1919.

AVEY, Gillian. "The Puritans and their Heirs," in: Gillian Avey and Julia Brigs (eds.), *Children and Their Books. A Celebration of the Work of Iona and Peter Opie.* Oxford: Clarendon, 1989.

CARPENTER, Humphrey and PRICHARD, Mari. *The Oxford Companion to Children's Literature.* Oxford: Oxford University Press, 1984.

COHEN, Morton N. *Rider Haggard. His life and Works.* New York: Walker, 1960.

DARTON, F.G. Harvey. *Children's Books in England. Five Centuries of Social Life.* 2nd ed. Cambridge: Cambridge University Press, 1966.

DEMOLINS, Edward. *Anglo-Saxon Superiority: To What It Is Due* (A quoi tient la supériorité des Anglo-Saxons?), translated by Louis Bert Lavigne. London: Leadenhall, 1898-9.

ETHERINGTON, Norman. *Rider Haggard.* Boston: Twayne, 1984.

FENN, George Manville. *George Alfred Henty. The Story of an Active Life.* London: Blackie, 1907.

GROSS, John and SPRINGHALL, J.O. "The Mystique of Empire" in: Stephen W. Sears. *The Horizon History of the British Empire.* American Heritage, 1973; pp. 295–301.

HANDY, Robert T. (ed.). *The Holy Land in American Protestant Life 1800–1948.* New York: Arno Press, 1981.

HARRISON, J.F.C. *The Second Coming: Popular Millenarianism 1780–1850.* London, 1979.

HAVILAND, Virginia. *The Travelogue Storybook of the Nineteenth Century. A Caroline Hewins Lecture.* Boston: Horn, 1950.

HUTTENBACK, Robert A. *The British Imperial Experience.* New York: Harper & Row, 1966.

KARK, Ruth. *American Consuls in the Holy Land, 1832–1914.* Jerusalem: Magnes, 1994.

KATZ, Wendy R. *Rider Haggard and the Fiction of Empire. A Critical Study of British Imperial Fiction.* Cambridge: Cambridge University Press, 1987.

KIEFER, Monica. *American Children Through Their Books 1700–1835.* Philadelphia: University of Pennsylvania Press, 1970.

LANDON, George P. *Victorian Types, Victorian Shadows: Biblical Typology in Victorian Literature, Art and Thought.* Boston, 1980.

MEIGS, Carolina (ed.) et al. *A Critical History of Children's Literature. A Survey of Children's Books in English.* Revised ed. New York: Macmillan, 1969.

MELMAN, Billie. *Women's Orients: English Women and the Middle East, 1718–1918. Sexuality, Religion and Work.* Ann Arbor: University of Michigan Press, 1992.

MUIR, Percy. *English Children's Books 1600–1900.* London: Blatsford, 1954.

NATIONAL UNION CATALOG. Pre-1956 Imprints. London: Mansell & American Library Association, 1975.

RAE, W. Fraser. *The Business of Travel. A Fifty Years' Record of Progress.* London: Thos. Cook & Son, 1891.

RAMSAY, Thomas. *The Life and Literary Remains of Barbara Hofland.* London: Cleaver, 1849.
——— . *Memoir of the Life and Literary Remains of Mrs. Hofland.* London: Arthur Hall, Virtue, & Co., 1850(?).

RÖHRICHT, Reinhold. *Bibliotheca Geographica Palæstinæ. Chronologisches Verzeichniss der auf die Geographie des heiligen Landes bezüglichen Literatur von 333 bis 1878 und Versuch einer Cartographie.* Berlin: Reuther, 1890.

ROSENBACH, Abraham Simon Wolf. *Early American Children's Books 1682-1847, with bibliographical descriptions of the books in his private collection.* Foreword by A. Edward Newton. Portland, Me.: Southward Press, 1933.

SAID, Edward W. *Orientalism.* New York: Vintage Books, 1979.

ST. JOHN, Judith (ed.). *The Osborne Collection of Early Children's Books.* Vol.I, 1566-1910; vol.II, 1476-1910. Toronto: Toronto Public Library, 1958, 1975.

SHEPHERD, Naomi. *The Zealous Intruders: The Western Rediscovery of Palestine.* London, 1987.

SMITH, Elva S. *The History of Children's Literature,* Revised and enlarged edition by Margaret Hodges and Susan Steinfist. Chicago: American Library Association, 1980.

STEVENSON, Robert Louis. *A Child's Garden of Verses.* Complete Edition. Racine: Whitman, 1931.

STINTON, Judith (ed.). *Racism and Sexism in Children's Books.* 1979.

THORNTON, A. P. *The Imperial Idea and Its Enemies. A Study in British Power.* London: Macmillan, 1959.

THWAITE, M. F. *From Primer to Pleasure. An Introduction to the History of Children's Books in England From the Invention of Printing to 1900, with a Chapter on Some Developments Abroad.* London: Library Association, 1963.

TOBLER, Titus. *Bibliographia Geographica Palæstinæ. Kritische Uebersicht gedruckter und ungedruckter Beschreibungen der Reisen ins Heilige Land.* Amsterdam: Meridian, 1964 (original edition: 1867).

VOGEL, Lester I. *Zion as Place and Past: An American Myth: Ottoman Palestine in the American Mind Perceived Through Protestant Consciousness and Experience.* Ph.D. dissertation, George Washington University, 1984.

—— . *To See a Promised Land. Americans and the Holy Land in the Nineteenth Century.* University Park, PA: Pennsylvania State University Press, 1993.

C. Juvenile books on the Holy Land and adjacent regions
(Works mentioned in the text and appearing in Part A. of the Bibliography are starred *.)

* ABBOTT, Jacob [1803-1879]. *History of King Richard the First of England.* New York: Harper, 1857. Engravings, 16mo viii 336 pp.
    (And several subsequent editions.)

* ADAMS, John (Reverend) [1750?-1814]. Excerpts from the writings of Baron de Tott, Mme. de Savary, Lady Montagu, and others on countries of the Middle East, in: *The Flowers of Modern Travels; being Elegant, Entertaining and Instructive Extracts,*

Selected from the Works of the Most Celebrated Travellers, etc. Intended chiefly for Young People of both Sexes. Boston: John West, 1797; 2 vols. 16mo 324 pp., 312 pp.
(And under slightly different titles in subsequent editions, some augmented, and in other formats, in 3 vols., etc. published in London: Kearsley, Darton & Harvey, 1799; Boston: For the Subscribers, 1816; Baltimore: M. Stewart, 1834.)

ADAMS, William Taylor (Oliver Optic) [1822–1897]. *American Boys Afloat, or Cruising in the Orient.* Boston: Lee & Shepard, 1893. Illustr. 12mo xi 343 pp.
——— . *Asiatic Breezes, or Students on the Wing.* Boston: Lee & Shepard, 1895. Illustr. 12mo xiii 361 pp.

* ALEXANDER, Barbara (Mrs. Hutton). *Heroes of the Crusades.* London: Giffith & Farran, (1868). Illustr. by P. Priolo, 12mo 319 pp.
(also American edition: New York: Whittaker, 1891. 318 pp.)
* ——— . *Tales of the Saracens.* London: Giffith & Farran, 1890. Illustr., 12mo 308 pp.

* ALEXANDER, James Waddell [1804–1859]. *Uncle Austin and His Nephews or, The Scripture Guide; being a Familiar Introduction to the Study of the Bible.* Philadelphia: American Sunday School Union, 1838. Illustr. 24mo 263 pp.

* ANDREWS, Jane [1833–1887]. "Gemila and Alee, the Child of the Desert " pp. 24–44, in: *The Seven Little Sisters Who Live on the Round Ball That Floats in the Air.* Boston: Ticknor & Fields, 1861. Illustr. 12mo. 119 pp.
(Also New Edition: Boston: Ginn, 1888, 1916, 1924. 16mo.)
* ——— . "What Was Gemila Doing All This Time" pp. 57–90, in: *Each and All; or, How the Seven Little Sisters Prove Their Sisterhood.* Boston: Lee & Shepard: 1877. Illustr, 16mo 142pp.
(And other editions: Boston: Ginn, 1877, 1885.)

(ANONYMOUS). *An Historical Geography of the Holy Land. With Some Notices of Other Countries Mentioned in the Old and New Testament, Compiled from the Sacred Volume and Illustrated by the Researches of Modern Travellers.* Dublin: White, 1832. 24mo iv 166 pp.

(ANONYMOUS). *Holy Land, Panorama for the Young.* London: Nelson, 1855. 4to.

(ANONYMOUS). *Le jeune voyageur dans la Syrie, l'Arabie, et la Perse.* Toulouse: Société des Livres Religieux, 1854. Wood engravings, 16mo 454 pp.

* (ANONYMOUS). *The English in Egypt with a Full and Descriptive Life of General Gordon, the Hero of Khartoum and Other Pioneers of Freedom. Together with Graphic Narratives of the Lives and Adventures of Lord Wolseley, Stewart, Burnaby, Horatio Nelson, Abercromby, Sidney Smith, Sir John Moore, Bruce, and other World-famous Heroes.* London: Sangster, (1886). 124 wood engravings & colored portraits from photos, 8vo viii 502 pp.

(ANONYMOUS). "Voyage to the Shores of the Dead Sea" in a Russian magazine for children, 1854, no. 13–5; and in: Rasinas, A., *Voyages to Different Countries of the World,* St. Petersburg, 1860, pp. 145–198.

APPEL, Theodore [1823–1907]. *Letters to Boys and Girls About the Holy Land and the First Christmas at Bethlehem.* Reading, Penna.: D. Miller, 1886. Front. map, plates, 12mo vi 155 pp.

APPLETON, Victor. *Don Sturdy in the Tombs of Gold, or, The Old Egyptian's Great Secret.* New York: Grosset & Dunlap, 1925. Illustr. by Walter S. Rogers, 12mo iv 214 pp.

BARTLETT, William Henry [1809–1854]. *Scripture Sites and Scenes, from Actual Survey, in Egypt, Arabia, and Palestine.* London: Hall, Virtue, ca. 1851. Engravings, woodcuts, maps, 8vo.

* BELL, William Dixon. *The Sacred Scimiter.* Chicago: Goldsmith, 1938. 12mo 252 pp.

BERTAL, Joseph. "De Constantinople à Jérusalem." Series of articles in: *Moniteur de la jeunesse, Journal de la famille illustré.* 1865: 73, 105, 135, 168, 201, 230, 262, 294; 1866: 13, 53, 84, 115, 151, 179, 209, 240, 273, 303, 336, 373.

BERTHON, A. *Bérénice ou le pèlerinage à Jérusalem.* Tours: Bibliothèque des écoles chrétiennes, 1846. 8vo.
    (And 2nd edition 1857; 5th edition 1863; 6th edition 1867.)

BEWSHER, Mrs. M.E. *Mischief-makers; or the Story of Zipporah; A Tale of the Times of Herod the Great.* London & Sydney: Griffith, Farran, Okedan, Welsh, [1891]. Illustr. by P. Priolo, 12mo xii 324 pp.
    (Also as: BEWSHIR, M.E. *Zipporah, the Jewish Maiden.*)

BLAKE, Isabel M. *Fez and Turban Tales.* New York: Interchurch Press, 1920. Photos, 12mo viii 115 pp.

BONAR, Andrew A. *Palestine for the Young.* London: Religious Tract Society, n.d. (ca. 1870). Illustr. map 12mo 368 pp.

* BOWMAN, Anne. *The Young Nile Voyagers.* London: Routledge, n.d. (1868). Illustr. by J.B. Zwecker, 16mo viii 440 pp.

BRERETON, Frederick Sadleir [1872–1957]. *On the Road to Bagdad, A Story of Townshend's Gallant Advance on the Tigris.* London: Blackie, 1917. Illustr. by Wal Paget, 12mo 384 pp.
    (Also 1929 edition.)
—— . *From the Nile to the Tigris; A Story of Campaigning from Western Egypt to Mesopotamia.* London: Blackie, 1918. Illustr. by Frank Gillett, 12mo 330 pp.
* —— . *With Allenby in Palestine.* London & Glasgow: Blackie, (1920). Illustr. by Frank Gillett, 8vo 287 pp.

BUCHAN, John [1875–1940]. *Greenmantle.* New York: George Doran, (1915). 12mo 345 pp.
    (And many subsequent editions.)

* BUTTERWORTH, Hezekiah [1839–1905]. *Zigzag Journeys in the Levant, with a Talmudist Story-Teller. A Spring Trip of the Zigzag Club Through Egypt and the Holy Land.* Boston: Estes & Lauriat, 1886. Illustr. 8vo 304 pp.

* CARPENTER, Frances [1890–19   ]. *Our Little Friends of the Arabian Desert, Adi and Hamda*. New York, Boston, etc.: American Book Co., 1934. Illustr. by Curtiss Sprague, 12mo 232 pp.
    (Also 1951 edition.)

* CHAMBERLAIN, George Walter [1859–19   ]. "A New England Crusade," *New England Magazine* 36 (1907) 2: 195–207.

* CHAMPNEY, Elizabeth Williams [1850–1922]. *Three Vassar Girls in the Holy Land*. Boston: Estes & Lauriat, 1892.

* ——— . "10th Transformation—to an Egyptian Child" and "20th Transformation—to a Syrian Girl—Damascus" in: *The Bubbling Teapot, A Wonder Story* by "Mrs. Lizzie W. Champney." Boston: Lothrop, n.d. (1886). Illustr. 12mo 266 pp.
    (Also 1893 edition, with 12 illustr. by Walter Satterlee, 8vo 266 pp.)

* CHANCE, Lulu Maude. "Ahmed, the Arabian Boy" pp. 66–81, in: *Little Folks of Many Lands*. Boston, New York, Chicago, London: Ginn, 1904. Illustr. 16mo 112 pp.
    (Also 1932 edition.)

* CHAPLIN, Fannie P. and HUMPHREY, Mrs. Frances A. "Zumetta" (a little Arab girl) pp. 7–18; "Muggerditch's Trowsers" (a little Turkish boy) pp. 31–38; "Little Folks in Egypt" pp. 50–58, in: *Little Folks of Other Lands*. Boston: Lothrop, Lee & Shepard, 1882. Illustr. 16mo vi 204 pp.

* CHARLTON, Lionel Evelyn Oswald (Air Commodore) [1879–1958]. *Near East Adventure*. London: Nelson, n.d. (1934). Illustr. by Ernest Ratcliff, 8vo vii 247 pp.

CURLEWIS, Constance F. *Our Little Armenian Cousin*. Boston: Page, (1907?).

DOUGLAS, Amanda Minnie [1837–1916]. *Heroes of the Crusades*. Boston: Lothrop, Lee & Shepard, ca. 1890. Illustr. 8vo.

* DOUGLAS, Hester. *The Land Where Jesus Christ Lived*. London: Nelson, 1890. Fold-out view of Nazareth, 12mo 303 pp.
    (Also 1894 edition of London, Edinburgh, New York.)

* DRAPER, Rev. Bourne Hall. *Bible Illustrations; or, A Description of Manners and Customs Peculiar to the East, Especially Explanatory of the Holy Scriptures*. London: Harris, 1831. Illustr. 24mo 256 pp.
    (And second edition, London: Harris, 1833; and American editions "by the Author of 'Peter Parley's Tales' with many improvements": Baltimore, 1; Philadelphia: Coperthwait, 1832; Boston: Carter & Hendae, 1832; Boston: Clapp & Broader, 1834; New York: Peasles, 1835. Both Boston editions contain the statement that they were copyrighted by Samuel G. Goodrich ["Peter Parley"] but the work is not included in Goodrich's list of his works in his *Recollections of a Lifetime*, and is not the same work as *Peter Parley's Book of Bible Stories*.)

DUCKWORTH, Rev. Canon Henry Thomas Forbes [1868–19   ]. *The Holy Land*.

London, Paris, New York: Tuck & Sons, (1904). Map, illustr. by W.J. Webb ("from original drawings painted in Palestine"), folio 36 pp.

* EDDY, Daniel Clarke [1823–1896]. *Walter's Tour in the East. Walter in Egypt.* New York: Sheldon, 1863. Illustr. 16mo 222 pp.

* ——— . *Walter's Tour in the East. Walter in Jerusalem.* New York: Sheldon, 1863. Illustr. 16mo 220 pp.

* ——— . *Walter's Tour in the East. Walter in Samaria.* New York: Sheldon, 1864. Illustr. 16mo 223 pp.

* ——— . *Walter's Tour in the East. Walter in Damascus.* New York: Sheldon, 1864. Illustr. 16mo 220 pp.

    (Also published New York: Crowell, 1864. 12mo)

* ——— . *Walter's Tour in the East. Walter in Constantinople.* New York: Sheldon, 1864. Illustr. 16mo 222 pp.

    (Also published by New York: Crowell, 1864. 12mo.)

* ——— . *Walter's Tour in the East. Walter in Athens.* New York: Sheldon, 1865. Illustr. 16mo 226 pp.

——— . *Rip Van Winkle's Travels in Asia and Africa by Rupert Van Wert.* New York: Crowell, 1882. Illustr. 12mo 314 pp.

* ——— . (Rupert Van Wert). *Van Wert's Travels in Asia and Africa.* Chicago and New York: Belford, Clarke, 1884. Illustr. 12mo 314 pp.

——— . *Young Folks' Travels in Asia and Africa.* Chicago: Belford-Clarke, 1890.

EDGAR, John George [1834–1864]. *The Crusades and the Crusaders.* London: Ward, Lock & Tyler, (1859). Illustr., frontispiece, 16mo vii (I) 408 pp.

    (And American edition: Boston: Ticknor & Fields, 1860. Illustr. by Julian Portch, 16mo vii [I] 380 pp.)

——— . *The Crusades and the Crusaders. Great Men and Gallant Deeds.* Boston: Lee & Shepard, n.d. ("Patriotic Series for Boys and Girls"). vii 380 pp.

    (And another edition in the "Jutland Series": Boston: Lee & Shepard, 1868. Illustr. 16mo 380 pp.)

——— . *The Boy Crusaders: A Story of the Days of St. Louis.* London: Cassell, Petter & Galpin, 1865. Illustr. by R. Dudley, 283 pp. Pls. sm. 8vo.

* EVERARD, William. *Sir Walter's Ward. A Tale of the Crusades.* London: Blackie, 1888. Illustr. by Walter Paget, 12mo 288 pp.

    (And American edition: New York: Scribner's & Welford, [1889].)

FENN, George Manville [1831–1909]. *Yussuf the Guide, Or, The Mountain Bandits, Being a Story of Strange Adventures in Asia Minor.* London, Glasgow, Bombay: Blackie, (1886). Illustr. by John Schönberg, 8vo 852 pp.

    (Also 1897 edition; and American edition under the title: *Yussuf the Guide, Being the Strange Story of Travels in Asia Minor.* New York: Scribner's, 1897.)

——— . *In the Mahdi's Grasp.* London: Dean, 1935. Frontisp. 8vo 248 pp.

FILLEUL-DE PÉTIGNY, Clara. *Les jeunes voyageurs en Palestine.* Rouen: Mégard, 184?. 16mo 252 pp.

    (Also 1852 8vo, and 1859 editions.)

188

—— . *La Palestine ou une visite aux Lieux Saints.* Bibliothèque Morale de la Jeunesse. Rouen: Mégard, 1866. 8vo.

* FINNEMORE, John [1863-1928]. *Peeps at Many Lands—The Holy Land.* London: Black, 1908. Illustr. by John Fulleylove, map, 12mo viii 83 pp.
    (And subsequent edition: London: Adam & Black, 1911.)

FRENCH, Harry W. (Abd El Ardavan) [1854-   ]. *The Lance of Kanana. A Story of Arabia.* Boston: Lothrop, Lee & Shepard, 1892. Illustr. by Garrett, 12mo 172 pp.
    (And subsequent editions 1916, 1920, 1932.)

GALT, John (pseud. of author of *Letters From the Levant?*) [1779-1839]. *Popular Voyages and Travels: Comprising the Tour of Asia. Abridged for the Use of Schools and Young People.* London: J.& C. Adelard, 1830. 16mo vi 402 pp.

GAUCHERAUD, Hyppolite. *Pélerinage d'une jeune fille du canton d'Unterwalden à Jérusalem, dans les années 1828-1831.* 2nd ed. revue et considérablement augmentée. Paris: Vaton & Gaure, ca. 1836.

GENLIS, Stéphanie Félicité Ducrest de St. Aubin, Comtesse de [1746-1830]. *Théatre à l'usage des jeunes personnes,* par madame la comtesse de Genlis. Paris & Maestricht: Dufour & Roux, 1782.

* —— . *Hagar in the Desert.* Translated from the French for the use of Children. Worcester, Mass.: Isaiah Thomas, 1785. 16mo 32 pp.
    (Also published in Newbury-port, Mass., 1790.)

* (GLEE, Prof.). *A Journey Round the World, Including Interesting Adventures in Many Lands with Professor Glee and His Class of Young People in Their Travels; visiting the Historic and Famous Cities and Places of Europe, Asia, Africa, South America, Australia and Many Islands of the Atlantic and Pacific Oceans, including the New Possessions of the United States.* (Place not given): W.E. Scull, 1901. Illustr. 200 engravings, 8vo xxxii 417 pp.

*GOODRICH, Samuel Griswold [1793-1860]. *Peter Parley's Tales About Asia.* Boston: Gray & Bowen, Carter & Hendee, 1830. Illustr. 32mo 116 pp.

* GOODRICH-FREER, Adela M. (Mrs. Hans Henry Spoer). *Things Seen in Palestine.* London: Seely, Service, 1913.
    (And an American edition.)

* —— . *Things Seen in Palestine.* New and Revised Edition, London: Seely, Service, 1927. 18mo 157 pp.

    GREEN, Lenamay [1869-1952]. *A Girl's Journey Through Europe, Egypt, and the Holy Land.* Nashville: Publishing House of the M.E. Church South, Printed for the Author, 1889. Illustr. 12mo 400 pp.
    (Also edition of 1890.)

* (GREGG, Jarvis) [1808-1836]. *Selumiel, or, A visit to Jerusalem; and the Most Interesting Scenes in and Around it. A.D. 40.* Philadelphia: American Sunday School Union, 1833. Illustr. 24mo 225 pp.

* HACK, Maria [1777-1844]. *Oriental Fragments.* London: Harvey & Darton, 1828. Plate, 16mo xi 140 pp.
(Also American edition — Philadelphia: T. Kite, 1829. 16mo 114 pp.)

* HAGGARD, Henry Rider [1856-1925]. *Pearl-Maiden, a Tale of the Fall of Jerusalem.* New York: Collier, 1902. Illustr. by Byam Shaw 12mo vii 463 pp.
(And subsequent London, New York, Toronto, and Leipzig editions.)

* ——— . *The Brethren; A Romance of the Time between the Second and Third Crusades.* London, Paris, New York, Melbourne: Cassel, 1904. 12mo viii 342 pp.
(Also, Leipzig: Tauchnitz, 1904.; 2 vols.; New York: Bunt (1904); illustr. 12mo. 411 pp.; New York: Mc Clure, Phillips & Co., 1904, illustr. by H.R. Miller, 12mo 411 pp.; and subsequent editions.)

* HALE, Edward Everett [1822-1909] & Susan HALE [1833-1910]. *A Family Flight over Egypt and Syria.* Boston: Lothrop, 1882. Illustr. 8vo 389 pp.
(And 2nd edition.)

HALE, Lucretia Peabody [1820-1900]. "The Peterkins Talk of Going to Egypt," *St. Nicholas Magazine,* February 1881.
——— . "Mrs. Peterkin in Egypt," *St. Nicholas Magazine,* August 1882.
——— . "Mrs. Peterkin Faints on the Great Pyramid," *St. Nicholas Magazine,* March 1883.

* HANSON, Helen Patten. *A Travel Book for Juniors.* New York, Cincinnati, Chicago: Abingdon, 1921-1930. Maps, photos, 12mo 258 pp.

HARPER, Henry Andrew [1836-1900]. *Illustrated Letters to My Children from the Holy Land: Eastern Manners and Customs, Depicted in a Series of Sketches from Life.* London: Religious Tract Society, (1880). Illustr. 8vo 82 pp.
(And other editions: n.d. 12mo 108 pp.; [1905] with three colored plates by Walter J. Morgan, 88 pp.)

* HARRISON, F. Bayford. *Brothers in Arms. A Story of the Crusades.* London: Blackie, 1885. Illustr. by Gordon Browne, 8vo 244 pp.

* HARRY, Myriam (Mme. Emile Perrault-Harry) [1875-1958]. "La petite fille de Jérusalem" *La Petite Illustration.* Part 1 (54):14 March 1914; part 2 (56):28 March 1914; part 3 (58):11 April 1914; part 4 (60):25 April 1914. Illustr. by F. de Haenen 4to 128 pp.

* ——— . *La petite fille de Jérusalem.* Paris: Arthème Fayard, 1914. Preface by Jules Lemaître, 12mo 349 pp.
——— . *The Little Daughter of Jerusalem.* London: Dent, 1918.
(Also several subsequent French, English, German, and Danish editions.)

HAWES, Joel [1789-1867] (ed.). *The Manners and Customs of the Jews, and Other Nations Mentioned in the Bible.* First American Edition. Hartford: Benton, 1833. Illustr. with 120 e, 12mo vi 172 pp.
(Based on earlier English edition.)

* HAWKS, Francis Lister [1798-1866]. *Richard the Lion Hearted; Romance of Biography,*

Illustrated in the Lives of Historic Personages. New York: Dickerson, 1855. Illustr. 12mo 273 pp.

> (And a 2nd edition.)

* HENTY, George Alfred [1832–1902]. *Winning His Spurs; A Tale of the Crusades*. London: Low, Marston, Searle & Rivington, 1882. Illustr. 12mo 314 pp.

> (And subsequent English and American editions, undated and in 1888, 1891, 1892, 1893, 1898, and 1954. Also published under the titles: *The Boy Knight who Won his Spurs Fighting with King Richard of England; A Tale of the Crusades*. Boston: Roberts Bros., 1883, plus undated editions and one in 1891; *Fighting the Saracens; or, the Boy Knight*. Boston: Brown, 188?; and, *Fighting the Saracens; a Tale of the Crusades*. Boston: Brown, 1892.

* ———. *For the Temple; a Tale of the Fall of Jerusalem*. London: Blackie, 1887. Illustr. by Solomon J. Solomon, 12mo 370 pp.

> (And several other American and English editions, undated and in 1887, 1888, 1902, 1924, and 1955.)

* ———. *The Young Midshipman. A Story of the Bombardment of Alexandria*. London: Blackie, and New York, 1890. 12mo iii 283 pp.

> (And editions in 1891, 1902, and 1955. Also under the title: *A Chapter of Adventures Or, Through the Bombardment of Alexandria*. New York: Scribner's. Illustr. by W.H. Overend, n.d. Crown 8vo.)

* ———. *The Dash for Khartoum. A Tale of the Nile Expedition*. New York: Scribner's, 1891. Ten illustr. by Joseph Nash and John Schönberg, 12mo 382 pp.

> (And several other American and English editions, undated and in 1892 and 1902.)

* ———. *At Aboukir and Acre; a Story of Napoleon's Invasion of Egypt*. New York: Scribner, 1898. Illustr. by William Rainey, 12mo ix 331 pp.

> (And three subsequent English and American editions in 1899, 1903, and 1915?.)

* ———. *With Kitchener in the Soudan. A Story of Atbara and Omdurman*. London & Glasgow: Blackie, n.d. (1902?). Illustr. by William Rainey, 12mo 384 pp.

> (And Subsequent English and American editions in 1902, 1903, and 1905.)

HILLYER, Virgil Mores [1875–1931]. "The Land of the New Moon," "The Ship of the Desert," A 'Once-was' Country," "A Land Flowing with Milk and Honey, "The 'Exact Spots'," "The Garden of Eden," The Land of Bedtime Stories," "The Lion and the Sun," pp. 309–355, in: *A Child's Geography of the World*. New York, London: Century, 1929. Maps, Illustr. xvii 472 pp.

> (Also editions in 1930, 1935, 1936, 1940, and a revised edition by Edward G. Huey 1951.)

* HOFLAND, Barbara (Wreaks Hoole) [1770–1844]. *Alfred Campbell; Containing Travels in Egypt and the Holy Land*. London: Harris, 1825. Illustr. 16mo vii 231 pp.

> (Also American editions — Boston: Munroe & Francis, 1826; New York: Roorbach, 1828.)

* —— . *Alfred Campbell; or Travels of a Young Pilgrim in Egypt and the Holy Land*. New edition with additions. London: Newman, 1841.

> (And No. 2 in the "Hofland Library" series, London: Hall, Virtue, ca. 1853; 12mo.)

* —— . *The Young Pilgrim, or Alfred Campbell's Return to the East and his Travels in Egypt, Nubia, Asia Minor, Arabia Petræa, &c &c...* London: Harris, 1826. Illustr. 12mo xii 211 pp.

> (Also American editions — New York & Charleston: Roorbach, 1828; and Philadelphia: Kay, 1831. 16mo; and No. 13 in the "Hofland Library" series, London: Hall, Virtue, ca. 1853; 12mo.)

* —— (HOFFLAND). *Theodore, or the Crusaders. A Tale for Youth*. London: Harris, 1821. Frontisp., 16mo ii 184 pp.

> (At least seven London editions with the name spelt correctly, Hofland, by the same publisher, among them, 3rd edition 1824; 4th edition 1826, viii 215 pp.; 6th edition 1833, Illustr. vi 210 pp. Also: *London: Griffith & Farran, 1879, 16mo 128 pp. American editions: Boston: Munroe & Francis, 1824, 6 plates, 12mo 180 pp.; and under the title *Theodore; or the Crusades*, New York: Dutton [1886], 16mo 128 pp.)

* HOLLIS, Gertrude. *A Slave of the Saracen. A Tale of the Seventh Crusade*. London, Edinburgh, New York: Nelson, n.d. (ca. 1902). Color plates by Paul Hardy, 8vo 271 pp.

* —— . *Between Two Crusades. A Tale of A.D. 1187*. London: Society for the Promotion of Christian Knowledge, (1908). Illustr. by Adolf Thiede, 8vo 247 pp.

> (American edition: New York: Gorham.)

—— . *The Land Where Jesus Lived*. London: Society for the Promotion of Christian Knowledge, (1912). Photo illustr., 12mo 160 pp.

> (American edition: New York: Gorham.)

HUMPHREY, Frances A. *Two Little Travellers*. Boston: D. Lothrop, 1883. Illustr. by George F. Barnes, 4o 30 pp.

* HUNT, Mrs. (Marion Edith) Holman [1847–1930]. *Children at Jerusalem: A Sketch of Modern Life in Syria*. London: Ward, Lock, n.d. (1881). Frontispiece, 12mo x 189 pp.

* HUNT, Sara Keables. *Yusuf in Egypt; and His Friends*. New York: American Tract Society, 1878. Illustr. 16mo 220 pp.

—— . *On the Nile; a Story of Family Travel and Adventure in the Land of Egypt*. London: Nelson, 1880.

HUTTON, Barbara. See ALEXANDER.

JAHONTOW, J. "Short Description of the Holy Land for Children who Study Sacred History". St. Petersburg, Weimar, 1856. 8vo 46 pp. (Russian).

* JAMIESON, Mrs. (late Miss Frances Thurtle). *Popular Voyages and Travels, throughout the Continent and Islands of Asia, Africa, and America: in which the Geography, the Character, and the Manners of Nations are Described; and the Phenomena*

of Nature, most worthy of Observation, are Illustrated on Scientific Principles. (Chapters I and II). London: Whittaker, 1820. Embellished with engravings, 16mo viii 478 pp.

* JOHNSON, Barton Warren [1833-1894]. *Young Folks in Bible Lands. Including Travels in Asia Minor, Excursions to Tarsus, Antioch and Damascus, and the Tour of Palestine.* St. Louis: Christian Publishing Co., 1892. Illustr. 12mo 400 pp.

JOHNSTONE, Mrs. Annie (Fellows) [1863-1931]. *Joel: A Boy of Galilee. A Story of the Time of Christ, which is one of the author's best-known books.* (Uniform with the "Little Colonel Books") Boston: Roberts, 1895. 10 illustr. by Victor A. Searles, 12mo 253 pp.

> (Another edition: Boston: L.C. Page, 1904. Illustr. by L.J. Bridgman, 12mo iv 253 pp., and a New Edition, 1918: 8vo.)

* JOHNSTONE, Mrs. Christian Isobel Christina Jane ("Aunt Jane") [1781-1857]. *The Wars of the Jews as Related by Josephus, Adapted to the Capacities of Young Persons.* London: Harris, 1823. Illustr. by 24 engravings after original designs by Mr. Brooke, 16mo xii 215 pp.

> (And 2nd English edition 1824, and American edition Boston: Munroe & Francis, 1826.)

JONES, Eli [1807-1890] and Sybil [1808-1873]. *Eastern Sketches: Notes of Scenery, Schools. and Tent Life in Syria and Palestine* by Ellen Clare Miller. Edinburgh, 1871.

JORGENSEN, O. *Vandringer i det hellige Land for Ynglinger og Pigerovs.* 1847.

* KALEEL, Mousa J. [1892-19]. *When I was a Boy in Palestine.* Boston: Lothrop, Lee & Shepard, 1914. Photo illustr., 12mo 152 pp.

KELLY, R. Talbot [1861-1934]. *Peeps at Many Lands. Egypt.* London: A. & C. Black, 1908. Illustr. by author, map, 12mo vii 87 pp.

> (And several subsequent editions in 1909, 1910, 1912, etc.)

* KING, Marian. *Amnon: A Lad of Palestine.* New York: Behrman, 1931. Illustr. by Elizabeth Enright, 12mo 96 pp.

> (Reprinted in 1945.)

KINGSLEY, Florence Morse. *Titus a Comrade of the Cross.* Elgin, Ill.: David C. Cook: 1894. Illustr., sm. 8vo 96 pp.

> (Also editions of 1895 and 1897.)

—— . *Stephen. A Soldier of the Cross.* Philadelphia: H. Altemus, 1896. Illustr. 12mo 369 pp.

* KNIGHT, Susan G. *Ned Harwood's Travels. Ned Harwood's Visit to Jerusalem.* Boston: Lothrop, 1888. Illustr. 8vo 286 pp.

* KNOX Thomas Wallace [1835-1896]. *The Boy Travellers. Adventures of Two Youths in a Journey to Egypt and the Holy Land.* New York: Harper, 1883. Illustr. maps, 8vo 438 pp.

* —— . *Boy Travellers in the Levant. Adventures of Two Youths in a Journey through*

Morocco, Algeria, Tunis, Greece and Turkey, with Visits to the Islands of Rhodes and Cyprus, and the Site of Ancient Troy. New York: Harper, 1894.

LEE, James Wideman [1849-1919]. *The Romance of Palestine: a History for Young People containing over One Hundred and Fifty Original Photographs and Pen Pictures...* St. Louis, 1897.

* LEVINGER, Elma Ehrlich. *Pilgrims to Palestine and Other Stories.* Philadelphia: Jewish Publication Society of America, 1940. Illustr. by M. Keller, 12mo x 274 pp. (Reprinted in 1944.)

* (LEYELL, Henry). *A Run Round the World or The Adventures of Three Young Americans. The Descriptive and Humorous Narrative of a Trip from New York to India and Back, in 1885-86, Embracing the Atlantic Voyage, England, France, the Rhine, Switzerland, Northern Italy, Austria, Servia, Bulgaria and Eastern Roumelia at the Time of the Late War, Turkey, the Black Sea, the Caucasus, the Caspian Sea, the Russian Trans-Caspian Region with its Railroad, Persia, Afghanistan, India, the Suez Canal Route, Egypt, the Holy Land, the Mediterranean Ports, etc.* Boston: De Wolfe, Fiske, 1891. Illustr. 300 engravings, crown-8vo viii 312 pp.
>(Published earlier as: *Amusing Adventures, Afloat and Ashore, of Three American Boys....* New York: Mrs. F. Leslie's Publishing House, 1886.)

MACDUFF, John Ross [1818-1895]. *Story of Bethlehem. A Book for the Young.* 2nd ed. London: Nisbet, 1859. Illustr. 8vo 136 pp.

(MACLEOD, Norman) [1812-1872]. *Half Hours in the Holy Land; Travels in Egypt, Palestine, Syria. An abbreviated reprint of the author's Eastward* by Annie C. Macleod. (The Half hour library of travel, nature, and science for young readers.) London: Isbister, 1885. Illustr. 12mo x 341 pp.
>(And several subsequent New York and London editions.)

* MANSFIELD, Blanche (Mc Manus) [1869-19]. *Our Little Arabian Cousin.* Boston: Page, 1907. Illustr. by author, 12mo vi 93 pp.
* ———— . *Our Little Egyptian Cousin.* Boston: Page, 1908. Illustr. by author, 12mo vi 93 pp.

MARTINEAU, Harriet (ed.) [1802-1876]. *Traditions of Palestine.* London: Longman, Rees, Orme, Browne, and Green, 1830. 12mo 141 pp.
———— . *The Times of the Saviour.* Reprinted, after revision, from the English edition. Boston: Bowles, 1831. 12mo 132 pp.
* ———— . *Traditions of Palestine: Times of the Saviour* New Edition. London: Routledge, 1870. 12mo xii 172 pp.
>(And other editions.)

MAY, Karl Friedrich [1842-1912]. *Durch Wüste und Harem, Von Bagdad nach Stambul, Orangen und Datteln, Im Lande des Mahdi,* and others, by a number of publishers in Germany and Austria between 1880 and 1900, and very many reeditions to this day.

MAZURE, M.P.A. *Le portefeuille du jeune amateur de la nature, de l'histoire et de l'art, ou description méthodique des sites et des monuments les plus remarquables dans les cinq parties du monde. Asie.* Paris: LeHuby, 1842. Engravings, 16mo 312 pp.

* McKENZIE, Edwin R. *Chronicles of Edwin R. McKenzie.* Indian River, Maine: unpublished manuscript, 1867.

MILLER, Elizabeth. *The City of Delight. A Love Drama of the Siege and Fall of Jerusalem.* New York: Grosset & Dunlap, 1908. Illustr. by F.X. Leyendecker, 12mo 448 pp.

MOCKLER-FERRYMAN, Lt.-Col. A.F. *The Golden Girdle.* London: Black, ca. 1907. Illustr. by Allan Stewart, lge. crown 8vo.

* MOFFETT, Cleveland [1863–1926]. *The Land of Mystery.* New York: Century, 1913. Illustr. from paintings and photos, 12mo x 413 pp.

* MORRIS, Robert [1818–1888]. *Youthful Explorers in Bible Lands: A Faithful Account of the Scenery, Ruins, Productions, Customs, Antiquities, and Traditions of Scriptural Countries; as Youthful Pens Would Describe Them, Joppa and Jerusalem, prepared and published under the auspices of* "The Scholar's Holy Land Exploration" of the United States. Chicago: Hazlitt & Reed, 1870. Illustr. and map, 8vo 224 pp.

> (And subsequent editions: 2nd ed., Chicago: Lakeside Press, 1871; and under another title:

—— . *Bible Witnesses from Bible Lands. Verified in the Researches of the Explorers and Correspondents of the American Holy Land Exploration, presenting a faithful account of the scenery, ruins, productions, customs, antiquities, and traditions of Bible lands,* [By] Robert Morris, John Sheville, Rolla Floyd [and] Samuel Hallock. New York: American Holy Land Exploration, 1874. Illustr. and map, 8vo 174 pp.

NORWAY, George. *Hussein the Hostage: Or, A Boy's Adventures in Persia.* London: Blackie, 1891. Illustr. by John Schönberg, Cr. 8vo.

> (Also other editions.)

OBER, Fred A. [1849–1913]. *The Knockabout Club in North Africa.* Boston: Estes & Lauriat, 1890. Illustr. 8vo 240 pp.

* OSBORN, Henry Stafford [1823–1894]. *The Little Pilgrims in the Holy Land.* Philadelphia: Challen, 1861. Illustr. 16mo viii 298 pp.

* PEPLOE, Annie (Molyneux) (Mrs. J.B. WEBB) [1805–1880]. *Naomi; or, The Last Days of Jerusalem.* London: Ward, Locke & Bowden, 1840. Frontispiece, 12mo 351 pp.

> (And many subsequent editions and revisions to 1899, among them the 17th "New Edition" with new Preface and illustr. by Gilbert and Bartlett; and a sumptuous one with mounted photographic illustrations after drawings by David Roberts: London: Routledge, 1872, Imp. 8vo 407 pp.; and including Finnish [1879], Danish [1899], Yiddish [1905], German [1906 and 1928], and Icelandic [1929] translations.)

* —— . *The Travels and Adventures of Charles Durand: Showing the Manners and the Customs of Eastern Nations, by Mrs. J.B. Webb.* London: Dalton, 1847. Illustr. 16mo 262 pp.

PHILLPOTTS, Eden. *The White Camel*. London: Country Life, 1936. Illustr. by Sheikh Ahmed, 12mo vi 165 pp.

PORTER, Horace [1837–1921]. *Our Young Aeroplane Scouts in Turkey; or, Bringing the Light to Yusef*. Our Young Aeroplane Scouts Series. New York: Burt, 1919. Illustr. 12mo.

* PRIDHAM, Caroline (Mrs. L.G. Wait). *Peeps at Palestine and its People*. London: Morrish, ca. 1875. Illustr. 8vo 189 pp.

* RAIDABAUGH, P.W. [18 -]. *The Pilgrims; or, Uncle Joseph and Rollin Through the Orient*. Cleveland: Evangelical Association, 1887. Illustr. 12mo vii 353 pp.

* ROBINSON, Edward [1794–1863]. *A Dictionary of the Holy Bible, for the Use of Schools and Young Persons*. Boston: Crocker & Brewster, 1833.
  (And several subsequent editions.)

* ROLT-WHEELER, Francis [1876–1960]. *The Wonder of War in the Holy Land*. Boston: Lothrop, Lee & Shepard, 1919. 47 Illustr. from war photos and sketches, 12mo x 368 pp.

ROUSIER, L. (M. l'abbé). *Le jeune voyageur dans la Terre Sainte*. Limoges-Paris: Bibliothèque religieuse, morale, littéraire, 1844. 8vo.

ROY, Lillian Elizabeth (Baker) [1868–1932]. *Polly in Egypt*. New York: Grosset & Dunlap, 1928. Illustr. by H.S. Barbour, 12mo 212 pp.

RÜDIGER, Minna Waack [1841–1920]. *Durch das Heilige Land. Eine Reise durch's gelobte Land in Briefen für Jung und Alt*. Konstanz & Emmishofen: Hirsch, ca. 1898. Color and b/w illustr., 4to 17 pp.

SARGEANT, Anne Maria [1809–1852]. *Mamma's Lessons on the History and Geography of Palestine, and Other Places Mentioned in the Bible*. London. 1849. 16mo.

SCHOR, Frances R. *Echoes from Palestine*. London: The London Society for Promoting Christianity Amongst the Jews, 1910. Photo illustr., 12mo x 106 pp.

SCHUMM, Oskar. "Ein Ausflug nach dem See Genezareth. Reiseerinnerungen aus dem Heiligen Lande," in: Schanz, Frida (ed.). *Junge Mädchen. Ein Almanach*, 4th year. Bielefeld & Leipzig: Velhagen & Klasing, n.d. (1896?), pp. 288–304.

SCHWED, Fr. *Die Pilgerreise nach dem heiligen Lande oder: Gottlieb Brunner's und seiner Gefährten Schicksale und Erlebnisse im Orient. Eine unterhaltende und in Bezug auf biblische Geschichte und Geographie belehrende Erzählung für die Jugend und deren Freunde*. Leipzig: Wöller, 1844. Illustr. 8vo.
  (And 2nd edition "...*Unterhaltende und belehrende Erzählung für Jung und Alt*." 1856.)

* SCOTT, Sir Walter [1771–1832]. *Tales of the Crusades*. Edinburgh: Constable, 1825. 12mo. 4 vols.
  (And very many other editions and translations, among them:
* ——— . *The Talisman; a Tale of the Crusades*. Philadelphia: McKay, n.d. Preface by

The Hon. Mrs. Maxwell Scott of Abbotsford, 12 color illustr. from original drawings by Simon Harmon Vedder, 8vo xxi 389 pp.

SEWARD, A.W.M. *Gespräche eines Vaters mit seinen Kindern über das heilige Land, oder Geographie von Palästina in Unterredungen, mit beständiger Hinweisung auf die heilige Schrift und mit vielen lehrreichen Bemerkungen...* Hamburg: Nestler, 1846. 8vo.

SINGER, Miriam [1898-1989]. *Benni fliegt ins gelobte Land. Ein Buch für jüdische Kinder.* Wien & Jerusalem: R. Löwit, 1936. Illustr. by Franz Reisz, 8vo 208 pp.

* STABLES, William Gordon M.D., R.N. [1840-1910]. *For Cross or Crescent. The Days of Richard the Lion-Hearted. A Romance.* Glasgow & Birmingham: Hulbert, 1927. Illustr., crown 8vo 380 pp.

    (Another edition by London: Shaw; and a New Edition: London: Dean, 1936. 8vo 248 pp.)

* STILLE, Caroline (ed.). *Alfred Campbell, oder Reisen eines Jungen Pilgers nach Aegypten und dem gelobten Lande. Frei nach dem Englischen für die Jugend bearbeitet.* Hamburg: Campe, 1830. 8vo.

* STRATTON, Ella (Hines). *Our Jolly Trip Around the World with Captain Parker, or The Lucky Thirteen and Their Long Voyage of Discovery in Search of Knowledge visiting Japan, China, India, Persia, Arabia, Egypt, Turkey, Greece, Palestine, Sicily, Italy, Africa, Spain, Portugal, France, England, Belgium, Holland, Germany, Russia, Finland, Sweden, Denmark, Norway, Scotland, and Ireland including a brief history of the countries visited from the earliest times to the present day; wonderful sights; queer and quaint peoples; their habits, customs, etc.* Philadelphia: National Publishing Co., (1902). Illustr. from photos, 8vo xiii 246 pp.

STRAUSS, Gerhard Friedrich Abraham [1786-1863]. *Helon of Alexandria. A Tale of Israel in the Time of the Maccabees* with a prefatory note by Adolph Saphir, D.D. [1831-1891]. London: Religious Tract Society, n.d. (ca. mid-1860s). Illustr. 16mo 159 pp.

    (This work for "youthful readers" is based on the author's original German, *Helon's Wallfahrt nach Jerusalem hundert und neun Jahr vor der Geburt Unsers Herren.* Eberfeld: Büschler, 1820, and subsequently also under different titles: *Helon's Pilgrimage to Jerusalem. A Picture of Judaism in the Century which Preceded the Advent of Our Saviour;* and *The Glory of the House of Israel; etc.* in English, French, and Dutch in various editions from 1824 to 1875.)

* SWEETSER, Kate Dickinson [18 -1939]. "Stephen and Nicholas: Boy Crusaders" pp. 11-44; "David: the Shepherd Boy" pp. 56-90, in: *Ten Boys from History.* New York & London: Harper, 1910. Illustr. by George Alfred Williams, 4to 210 pp.

—— . *Peggy's Prize Cruise.* New York & Newark: Barse & Hopkins, 1925. Illustr. 8vo 313 pp.

TAYLOR, Isaac [1759–1829]. *Scenes in Asia, for the Amusement and Instruction of Little-Stay-At-Home Travellers.* Hartford, 1826. Illustr. map, 16mo vi 124 pp.
(Also published by Hartford: Andrus, 1830.)
———. *Scenes in Europe and Asia, for the Amusement and Instruction of Little-Stay-At-Home Travellers.* A New Edition. London: Harris, 1827. Illustr. map, 12mo vii 207 pp.

* THOMAS, Lowell Jackson [1892–1981]. *The Boys' Life of Colonel Lawrence.* New York & London: Century, 1927. Photo illustr., map, 12mo vii 293 pp.
(And subsequent editions New York & London: Appleton, 1938.)

TILLOTSON, John [ca.1830–1874]. *The Land of the Bible: Its Sacred Heroes and Wonderful Story.*

* (TILT, Charles) [1797–1861]. *The Boat and the Caravan; a Family Tour Through Egypt and Syria.* London: Bogue, 1847. Illustr. 8vo 443 pp.
(And 2nd edition 1849, xii 441 pp.; 3rd edition 1850, 16mo; and at least a 5th edition. Also German edition: *Das Boot und die Karawane, eine Familienreise durch Aegypten, Palästina und Syrien.* Nach der 5ten Auflage…aus dem Englischen übersetzt und mit Anmerkungen versehen von E.A.W. Himly. Leipzig: Schlicke, 1860. 8vo xviii 419 pp. Also a Dutch translation from German by A.A. Deenik. Haarlem: deErven Loosjes, 1861. 8vo.)

TRUPPER, H.A. *Uncle Allen's Party in Palestine.* Philadelphia: American Baptist Publication Society, 1898.

VAN DYKE, Henry [1852–1933]. *The Lost Boy.* New York & London: Harper, 1914. Illustr. by N.C. Wyeth, 16mo 69 pp.

VINCENT, John Heyl [1832–1920]. *Little Foot-prints in Bible Lands; or, Simple Lessons in Sacred History and Geography for the Use of Palestine Classes and Sabbath Schools. With Introduction by Rev. T.M. Eddy, D.D.* New York: Carlton & Porter, 1861. Illustr. 12mo 139 pp.; Baltimore: Methodist Book Depository, 1861. 8vo.

* WADE, Mary Hazelton (Blanchard) [1880–1936]. *Our Little Jewish Cousin.* Little Cousin Series; Boston: Page, 1904. Illustr. by L.J. Bridgman, 12mo vi 91 pp.
(11th impression, October 1925, with new Introduction.)
* ———. *Our Little Turkish Cousin.* Little Cousin Series. Boston: Page, 1904. Illustr. by L.J. Bridgman, 12mo ix 107 pp.
* ———. *Twin Travelers in the Holy Land.* New York: Stokes, 1919. Color frontispiece and photo illustr., map, 12mo v 115 pp.

WATSON, Henry Clay [1831–1869]. "Camp-Fire of the Nile," "Camp-Fire of Mount Tabor," Camp-Fire of Aboukir" pp. 97–122, in: *The Camp-Fires of Napoleon: Comprising the Most Brilliant Achievements of the Emperor and his Marshals.* Philadelphia: Porter & Coates, 1850. Illustr., 12mo x 448 pp.
(Also editions of 1854 and 1877; Philadelphia: Peck & Bliss, 1867.)

WEBB, Mrs. J.B. See above, under PEPLOE, Annie.

WHITHAM, G.I. *Sir Sleep-Awake and his Brother: A Story of the Crusades*. London: Blackie, ? . Illustr. by N. Tenison.

* WILLARD, Mary Frances [1867–19]. *Along Mediterranean Shores*. Boston: Silver, Burdett, 1914. Photo illustr., map, 12mo 269 pp.

WILSON, Sarah (Atkins). *Fruits of Enterprize Exhibited in the Travels of Belzoni in Egypt and Nubia, Interspersed with the Observations of a Mother to Her Children. To Which is Added a Short Account of the Traveller's Death*. By the author of "Relics of Antiquity" 5th ed. London: Harris, 1825. 16mo x 238 pp.

* WISE, Daniel [1813–1898]. *Boy Travelers in Arabia: or, From Boston to Bagdad: Including Pictures, Sketches, and Anecdotes of the Wandering Arabs, and of the City "of Good Haroun Alrashid"*. New York: Hunt & Eaton and Cincinnati: Cranston & Curts, 1893. Wood engravings, 12mo 278 pp.
> (Originally published New York: Phillips & Hunt, 1885.)

YONGE, Charlotte Mary [1823–1901]. *The Patriots of Palestine; a Story of the Maccabees*. New York: T. Whittaker, 1898. Illustr. by W.S. Stacey, 12mo x 203 pp.

* ———— . *The Prince and the Page; a Story of the Last Crusade*. London & Cambridge: Macmillan, 1866. Illustr. by R. Farren, 16mo vi (I) 256 pp.
> (And many subsequent editions: in 1880, Macmillan; 1881 and 1885, Boston: Lothrop, viii 9–369 pp.; new edition: 1883 and seven editions until 1911, London: Macmillan, with frontisp. by Adrian Stokes; 1925 and 1930, New York: Macmillan, illustr. by Marguerite De Angeli.)

ZWEMER, Amy Elizabeth (Wilkes). *Two Young Arabs; the Travels of Noorah and Jameel*. West Medford, Mass.: The Central Committee on the Study of Foreign Missions, 1926. Illustr. 12mo 216 pp.

* ZWEMER, Samuel Marinus [1867–1952]. *Childhood in the Moslem World*. New York: Revell, 1915. Illustr. 12mo 274 pp.

* ZWEMER, Samuel Marinus [1867–1952] & Amy Elizabeth (Wilkes). *Topsy Turvy Land; Arabia Pictured for Children*. New York & Chicago: Revell, 1902. Illustr. 12mo 124 pp.

* ———— . *Zigzag Journeys in the Camel Country. Arabia in Picture and Story*. New York: Revell, 1911. Photo illustr. 12mo 125 pp.

INDEX

saw a gentleman and lady in European dress dashing towards them over the rocky road.

"Who are they?" asked Harry.

"I don't know."

"Hallo, Mr. Tenant," cried Walter to the gentleman nearest him, "here comes two civilized beings."

"How can you tell whether they are civilized or uncivilized?"

"By their dress, — they are Europeans."

The gentleman and lady were now drawing near, and soon reined up their horses in the way.

"How far have you come?" asked the man.

"From Ramleh to-day."

"How many hours to Joppa?"

"About ten."

"Is the road good?"

"No; very bad."

A mutual understanding now took place. Our party told the man who they were, and he in turn told them he was an Englishman, who, with his wife, were seeing Palestine. Her face was sunny and cheerful through the rain, while his was moody and sour. After getting all the information they could, they drove on, the lady waving her hand in token of farewell.

"Isn't it good, Walter, to see a lady here in this country?" asked Harry.